Staff to Last!

"The Staff to Last! approach has transformed my team and the way we work together. Mine used to be a practice that seemed to eventually find its way to its destination but only after getting lost several times along the way. Working with Lauren is like installing a GPS system into your firm."

— Ron Greenberg, Greenberg & Rapp

Staff To Last!

For Financial Advisors Only:

How to build a staff that makes your clients HAPPY, your peers JEALOUS, and your wallet FAT

By

Lauren Farasati

iUniverse, Inc.
New York   Bloomington

Staff to Last!
For Financial Advisors Only: How to build a staff that makes
your clients HAPPY, your peers JEALOUS, and your wallet Fat

iUniverse books may be ordered through booksellers or by contacting:

iUniverse
1663 Liberty Drive
Bloomington, IN 47403
www.iuniverse.com
1-800-Authors (1-800-288-4677)

ISBN: 978-1-4401-1863-0 (pbk)
ISBN: 978-1-4401-1864-7 (ebk)

Printed in the United States of America

iUniverse rev. date: 3/13/2009

With gratitude

I'm a pretty good starter but not such a hot finisher. I owe a huge debt of gratitude to my son, Adam Farasati, who worked with me to structure the book and who dragged me across the finish line when the book was ninety percent done and I was procrastinating. He was a steadfast coach, cheerleader, and taskmaster. I could not love him more.

I also owe a huge thank you to my industry pre-readers. At different points in their careers and from different corners of the industry, each of these individuals has built a *gifted practice*. They were incredibly generous with their time, input and encouragement. Thank you, Bryan Sweet, Adam Stock and Brian Redders.

Finally, everything I've learned about leadership and management I learned from two men, Nick Horn and Ted Santon. Nick and Ted were partners in one of the industry's most successful and distinguished firms. They took a chance hiring me because I had never stayed with a job for longer than two years. I ended up spending twenty years working with them. What Ted and Nick taught me is that nothing matters unless you're growing people.

They never delegated a task without delegating a heap of confidence along with it. They made a huge fuss over my victories and quickly forgot my mistakes. They never let me think I could fail.

Every wonderful thing that has happened in my career I can trace right back to Nick and Ted.

Table of Contents

Introduction

If I asked you what you *love* about your job, what would you say? Most of the advisors I know would say, "Lauren, I love being in front of clients." "I love presenting ideas and explaining complex concepts." "I'm great at building relationships." "I enjoy crafting innovative technical solutions." "I love helping people in a meaningful way."

But if you picked up this book, like 99% of financial advisors I've ever met, you *do not* love management. In my twenty-five years in this industry, I've frequently heard advisors say, "Lauren, my staff isn't meeting my expectations," or worse, "Lauren, my backroom is killing me." But I've yet to hear a single one say, "Lauren, I just *love* management!"

If managing your practice is feeling less like a ball and more like a ball and chain, here's the good news. My name is Lauren Farasati, and what *I* love to do is help financial advisors grow their practices. I started my career in our industry in 1984, as the Operations Director at the San Francisco branch of New England Financial, managing staffing and operations. Then, during my twenty-years with Lincoln Financial Advisors, I served as Vice President of Operations for its largest regional office; helping advisors at all levels grow their practices by surrounding them with support services that freed them to concentrate on helping clients. In 2004, Lincoln Financial Advisors created a national internal consulting group called the Office of Practice Management. As Director, I developed a package of concepts, tools and systems to enable advisors to attract and retain top staff talent. And now, as creator of the coaching firm, *The Gifted Practice*, I work with many of the biggest and most successful financial services practices in the country, helping them create multi-million dollar revenues without drowning under the weight of management or client service.

And you know what I've learned after all these years in our industry? That every financial advisor is just *one great hire away* from being able to make their practice vision a reality. One great hire who can tenaciously process business. One great hire who will systematize your practice. One great hire who will eventually hire and train others. One great hire to free you to do what you love to do.

Many advisors earning millions of dollars have the exact same headaches as a first year financial advisor…what they want is to spend all their time in front of clients; what they end up doing is spending way too much time in the backroom. My objective in writing this book is to take what I've learned about building amazing support teams and share it with the many advisors I may not have the opportunity to work with personally.

You'll learn the roles every successful practice should have, from that first dynamite *Administrative Assistant* to the *Concierge* who will masterfully attend to your most valued clients. We'll discuss what roles your particular practice needs, from the advisor in their first year of business to the firm with hundreds of millions in assets under management. Then we'll find out how to get the right people in these roles, beginning with the initial internet posting to foolproof interview questions, right down to making the offer. Most importantly, you'll learn how to keep the great people you've found…how to train, how to reward, and how to lead. I believe one of the reasons I've been successful in this industry is because to understand staff, it helps to have been part of a few. And that's exactly what I was; for ten years, before I ever worked with advisors, I was an executive assistant, working for every type of boss imaginable. I understand the staffing relationship – as employee, as employer, and as coach – and I bring that experience to bear every day when I sit down with advisors and staff.

The best part is…it's simple. We don't need a lot of charts or graphs. After all, staffing is about people. And you're good with people. In fact, you're downright magical when it comes to dealing with clients. Very soon, dealing with your staff will be no different.

So read on! I'm about to do what I love doing…freeing you from your staffing woes, so that you have the time, the tools, and the energy to do what *you* love to do.

Your Dream Practice begins now.

The Roles

A Typical Practice

Let me talk to you about Bob.

Bob is a smart, bright-eyed young financial advisor, just finishing his first year in the business. It hasn't been a cakewalk...there's been a lot to learn; he works long hours, and he spends more time marketing than designing financial solutions. But he doesn't mind. Everyone tells him that's just how the industry is at first, and he sips his coffee and smiles, knowing things will get easier.

Soon, Bob is on his feet and can afford a little help, so he takes a fellow advisor's advice and hires Tina, a part-time assistant to help with the paperwork. This seems like a nice step forward. Tina is great with the paperwork, and she even brings him his coffee in the morning. The addition of Tina takes some of the burden off of Bob, but twenty hours a week doesn't take care of all the paperwork, let alone the marketing and investment planning that Bob still has to handle. He'd like a little more support, but that would require more income, which requires more clients, which he doesn't have yet.

But time passes, and after a few years in the industry Bob's client list has grown. He decides to make Tina a full-time employee. Again, this helps some, but there are still problems. Bob delegates some of the marketing and basic number-crunching to Tina, but he still only has one employee, and if she calls in sick or takes a vacation then the office quickly falls apart. And with the extra workload, Tina is now bugging Bob to get her some help.

Bob decides to hire Kyle, a part-time assistant for Tina. Once again, the extra set of hands helps in the short-term, but in the long run not a whole lot has changed. Tina's great with the paperwork, but not as marvelous with the marketing and analytical work that Bob has delegated to her. Bob ends up having to take back many of the projects he delegates if he wants them done right. Work is stressful and his doctor tells him to cut back on the coffee. But he soldiers on.

After ten years in the business, Bob finally has a substantial client list and realizes he needs someone more technical to help with planning and investment design. So he bites the bullet and hires Dave, a ParaPlanner. Finally, Bob believes his staffing problems have been resolved.

And for a while, it seems they have. For the first year or so things seem to be running better and more work gets done. But problems arise. The office is messy; there is confusion as to who is supposed to do what. And with each new employee Bob has layered on he is also layering on more management, which he hates. And despite adding an extra set of hands, Bob still works as much as ever, making him frustrated and cranky and, in turn, putting the staff in a bad mood. He notices people call in "sick" more often then they used to. Bob's not feeling that great either. He takes a swig of Maalox and hopes things will somehow get better.

But they don't. Tina quits. The office is in chaos, so Bob immediately hires someone to replace Tina, but it doesn't work out, so he replaces that assistant. Over the next few years he goes through an assistant every six months or so. The bad ones he fires, the good ones quit. Handling all this turnover – reading resumes, interviewing, let alone training these new people over and over again – is becoming a job in itself. Bob is annoyed that after years of investing time and money in staff, he has as many headaches as when he started.

Bob is convinced staffing is more problem than solution. He really can't afford new staff even if he wanted because his client list has reached a plateau. But he thinks he may have the answer. He brings in recent college grad, Tim, his buddy's son, to groom as a Junior Advisor. Tim can help get new clients and also take over some of the management Bob hates. Maybe one day Tim will even be able to buy him out. Bob smiles (for the first time in a while) at the prospect of someday leaving these daily headaches to someone else.

But alas, the junior isn't quite the missing puzzle piece Bob had hoped. Tim is a good advisor but he doesn't have any more management ability than Bob did. And Bob realizes he isn't as keen as he thought on mentoring this kid for the two or three years it will take to get him on his feet. The office remains chaotic, causing Tim to falter.

Bob throws up his hands, disappointed. He's not exactly miserable, but this just isn't how he envisioned his practice when he began fifteen years ago. He thought he'd like his job more. He thought he'd like his staff more. He thought he'd spend his days in front of clients, not dealing with backroom headaches. Bob tells what's-her-name at the assistant's desk to just skip the coffee from now on and bring him his Maalox in the morning.

I know - Bob's story is a downer. But the truth is I talk with people like "Bob" every day. Smart, hard-working advisors who fall out of love with their careers because of staffing frustrations. But here's the very good news. If you're just starting, you don't have to take the same road as Bob. And if you're already on the "Bob" road, there's time to get off.

We can learn from Bob. We can ask ourselves: Where did Bob go wrong? Why did our young friend first hire someone to help with paperwork, when what he really needed was help getting more clients? Why did he opt for one full time employee and not explore the benefits of two part-timers? Did it makes sense to keep adding extra hands without first having a vision of what roles they would be playing? Why is Bob spending so much time doing management, the thing he hates most? Come to think of it, could he have hired somebody to manage the staff for him? Would better planning have created a happier staff? Would a happier staff have been more likely to stay? Would one of those long-term employees emerged as a stronger associate than Tim? Would all of this have created a happier Bob?

This book will answer these questions and your frustrating and expensive staffing puzzle will become simple. I'll provide all the puzzle pieces - vision, systems, tools and templates – and show you, step-by-simple-step, how to assemble the puzzle.

And the biggest, most important puzzle piece is on the next page.

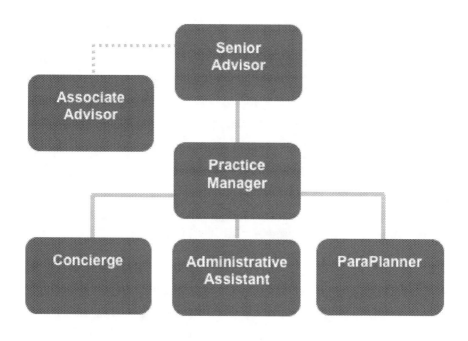

The Dream Team

To your left is a diagram of what I have dubbed *The Dream Team*.

Our poor friend Bob, the Financial Planner, had several problems with staffing, but, ironically (given his job title), the biggest was simply a lack of planning. As simple as this illustration may be, it would have spared Bob from career-long drains on his time, wallet, and psyche.

Bob didn't understand the simple truth my former boss, Ted Santon, reminded me nearly every day – "Kiddo, people change, but not much." Because of this, Bob continuously placed employees in roles that were poorly defined and that didn't play to the employees' strengths. This problem is rampant in our industry and accounts for the revolving door of staffing far too many advisors endure.

For every role in an advisory practice, there is a talent or package of talents that, when applied, will produce amazing results. I believe in the magic of task/talent congruity so completely that fully one third of this book is devoted to getting these matches right.

There are five fundamental and distinctly different support roles: **The Administrative Assistant** (organization and paperwork), **The ParaPlanner** (analytical and technical work), **The Concierge** (marketing), **The Practice Manager** (management), and **The Associate Advisor** (like you, but poorer). The more tightly you define a role, the more likely you are to find the right person to perform it. Conversely, the more you try to stretch people across roles, the more unhappy and unproductive they will be. The majority of advisors do not employ all these roles in their practices. But if you're going to get bigger and stronger than your competitors, you'll need a roadmap to guide that growth. So as we learn whom these key players in your practice are, and how they help you worry less and deal with clients more, keep in mind one thing. Whether you have already formed negative staffing expectations after years of disappointment, or are hoping to avoid such woes with your first employee, getting the train on the right track starts with one great hire. And for most of you, that one great hire is the subject of our next chapter.

The Administrative Assistant

If there were one person, one role, one single piece of the puzzle that I could wish for you to find, it would be a stellar **Administrative Assistant**. This role is as much the cornerstone of this book as it should be the cornerstone of your practice. Whether you will some day have a team of employees, or enjoy a well-run practice that requires only one employee, this is the hire that will have the most impact on your present and future success. If you hire the right person in this role, a feeling of serenity washes over you, the clouds part, and angels sing, *"You Are The Wind Beneath My Wings."* And if you hire the wrong person, you feel, well…sort of like you do now.

And who is the right person? I believe that there are two traits that make for a great Administrative Assistant, and if a candidate doesn't have both of these qualities in spades, they cannot, under any circumstances, be hired. End of story, no exceptions.

The Genes

You might be wondering why I confer such significance to a position that, at least historically, most would consider the entry-level spot in a financial practice. Well, there are a couple reasons. First, look at how much more complex the role of Administrative Assistant is in our industry than in others. In other industries, the Administrative Assistant is responsible for organizing meetings, handling phone calls, making travel arrangements and submitting expense books. In our industry, an Administrative Assistant will do all that, *plus* process paperwork for a myriad of products and companies, provide service to clients, fulfill compliance requirements, manage the schedule, and track revenue and commissions. They will be responsible for almost all the systems that support the practice and the client experience.

If this is the first or only support person in the practice he or she will be your "everything person" often working without external resources to guide and support. And as you might imagine, the most demanding aspect of the job won't be the handling of any one particular task, but the multitasking of all of them. That's what sets the job of Administrative Assistant in the financial services industry apart. This job is darn hard and to perform it successfully an individual must have one very specific talent that cannot be faked. They need **the organization gene**.

I call it a "gene" because I think it's the kind of trait that can't be learned, or taught…it just has to be in the DNA. Yes, a messy person can be trained to be tidy (for a while); someone might like a cluttered home but have no trouble keeping an organized desk at work. But this isn't whom you're going to hire. What we want is the person who is naturally driven to create organization out of chaos.

One thing I've noticed after years of observing truly organized people is the way they are with paper. It's a dead giveaway. Someone with the organization gene touches paper in a different manner than most people do. They don't just hold it…they *fondle* it. Yup, I agree, it's weird, but look for it. Maybe you've noticed people like this in the supermarket, groping guavas and caressing corn. These people are food lovers. Sure, I might squeeze the occasional melon to see if it's ripe, but these foodies really go nuts on their roughage. After ten minutes in the produce section, they look like they need a cigarette.

But I can't blame them. They've got the food lover gene. We need someone with the organization gene. The person with this gene doesn't have to be asked to be tidy, they just are. The organizational process…paper into stacks, stacks neatly paper-clipped, paper-clipped files labeled, labeled files into cabinets…isn't a chore for them. Heck, they do it with their recipes or baseball cards at home, just for fun. On the other hand, as much as we want a paper lover, we don't want a total perfectionist. There's too much to do in this job and it's never going to be perfect, and if you take time trying to make it perfect you're probably neglecting something else. Remember, we want the organization gene, not the obsessive-compulsive gene. True paper lovers handle these organizational tasks quickly, effortlessly, and with smiles on their faces.

Why all the fuss about organization? Two reasons. First, organization is probably a major area where *you* are lacking. A good assistant will balance that, bringing a sense of calm to a hectic and disorganized office environment. And two, it's the umbrella trait that will help your assistant multi-task all their responsibilities.

The second gene the administrative role requires is equally crucial.

An Administrative Assistant can be the most technically proficient person in the world…certainly there are a lot of smart and organized cookies out there that have the ability to do this job. But there's a quality that doesn't easily show up on paper, a requirement that a lot of advisors overlook when hiring. In fact, most advisors would be a little embarrassed to admit it was even something they were looking for. But it's nothing to be embarrassed about. In fact if a potential hire doesn't have it in their DNA, like the organization gene, you'll never feel truly supported.

We need someone with **the nurturing gene**. Someone who will enjoy looking after you. When we talk later in this book about what motivates people, we'll talk about what makes this person different. Most nurturing people are motivated by *intrinsic* needs, as opposed to the majority of advisors, who are motivated by *extrinsic* needs. What does that mean? Well, if you're like most advisors, you respond to incentives like money, prizes, and rewards. You'll gladly kill yourself trying to finish in the top 5% of your company to win a vacation to Cabo, even though most advisors in the top 5% of their company could easily afford the trip on their own. But that competition, that drive to win, and getting the shiny prize, that's what gets you going. But what gets an intrinsic person going is something totally different: A pat on the back, a smile on the face of a person they've helped, knowing that they're needed. These are the motivations for the person we're looking for.

Now, I've met advisors who say, "Oh yeah, Lauren, my assistant is like that. Whenever I ask her for something, she's on it. She never screws up anything I give her." But hang on…your standards seem a little low. Remember, an assistant is *supposed* to do things you ask them to do. That's their job! Do your clients say of you, "Oh, my financial advisor is great. He watches my money." Of course not. They expect more than just the bare minimum from you, and you should expect the same of your assistant. We're looking for someone who wants to exceed expectations, without being asked. This person sees you looking up a phone number and says "Don't worry, I've got that." When you say to your assistant "I have to pick up my watch from the jeweler. Call my three o'clock and let them know I'm running late," this person doesn't just acknowledge the task. She says "Don't worry about the watch, I'll get it. That way you'll have a little extra prep time."

That's the crux of it. This person is going to do everything they can to make sure you aren't thinking about anything other than your clients. From managing the office, to troubleshooting technology issues, to getting you your coffee in the morning. There, I've said it...getting you your coffee. I know that many people – perhaps even some who work with you – feel that expecting staff to perform personal tasks is antiquated and insulting. And yet that's the kind of thing a great Administrative Assistant does. By the way, the preponderance of financial advisors are men and the preponderance of Administrative Assistants happen to be women but the nurturing gene has nothing to do with gender. What we're talking about here is someone whose believes it's their job to support the advisor any way they can. Years after my assistant days, I was the Director of Operations for a large field office of Lincoln Financial Advisors and I still got my bosses coffee or grabbed them lunch. Why, you ask? Because, I, too, have the nurturing gene. It wasn't my job, and nobody asked me too. But they were my bosses and helping them made me feel good.

The Job

What does an Administrative Assistant do? We've gone over the basics, and discussed what it is to be an "everything" person. And later in this book, when we discuss *job descriptions*, we'll get into the nuts-and-bolts specifics of the job. But in offices where a single Administrative Assistant is not your only employee, there are many interesting and creative ways to utilize this role that can streamline and upgrade the infrastructure.

One of the most successful spins I have seen on this role comes from practices where investment and insurance support tasks are roughly equal. In many of these practices, the workload is so heavy that advisors will bring in one assistant, then another, and another, just like Bob did. But a very effective support alternative is to position one assistant as the *Investment Support Specialist* and the other as the *Insurance Support Specialist*, each one being responsible for soup-to-nuts support for their line of business. By doing this, you divide the workload approximately evenly between two Administrative Assistants, eliminate role confusion that can result from assistants supporting assistants, and boost ownership and accountability. Perhaps the biggest benefits are the increases in productivity and quality you get when you develop people in specialist roles.

Another variation for practices with multiple assistants involves dividing the labor based on *function*. To functionalize the administrative role, you might have one person being responsible for preparing and completing paperwork and a second responsible for pushing that paperwork through and dealing with underwriting, transfers and client communication.

Conclusion

You now have a picture of what a *"Dream Team"* Administrative Assistant looks like. Remember, we're looking for two things: organization and nurturing. If you are relaxed and confident going into a meeting, it's because you have a great person in this role. If returning to the office is something you look forward to, it's because you have a great person in this role. If all office worries great and small are being addressed, and your time is being spent in front of clients, it's because you have a great person in this role.

The ParaPlanner

You've said goodbye to paperwork, filing, and scheduling. You understand the role of the Administrative Assistant, the nurturing, organized individual who will relieve you of the daily stresses that suck up time you should be spending with clients. And for many practices, that's as far as the process needs to go. Your income or workload doesn't necessitate any more support, at least not right now.

But I need you to keep reading.

I need you to keep reading because things change. Your clients change, the industry changes, your practice changes. And while we can never know the future, we can certainly make reasonable predictions, and I'll make one right now. If you're good at what you do, work hard and hire the right people, your practice will grow and, along with it, your staffing needs. It may take one year or it may take ten. It may have already happened. Regardless, staffing is not something you want to be playing catch up with. This book is designed to prevent reactive staffing solutions. When you're done reading what's between these pages, I want you to have a full and fundamental understanding of staffing and have built a solid foundation on which to build your practice. That means not just knowing where you are, but also where you may be going. And with that in mind, let's turn our attention to the next possible weapon in your support arsenal, **The ParaPlanner**.

Unlike the Administrative Assistant role, the role of ParaPlanner can be trickier to delegate for one principal reason. This role, with its emphasis on analysis and number crunching, may represent work that you enjoy doing. You may even push this work to the top of the pile, to the detriment of prospecting. But your time needs to be spent in revenue producing activities so, let's get you out from behind the computer and take a look at the next set of invaluable "genes."

The Gene

You just sat down for the first time with the Coles. The data meeting went well. You come back to the office with a yellow pad full of data and a box full of investment statements. Between Mr. and Mrs. Cole, there are seventeen different accounts of every ilk, plus two to three accounts for each of the kids, plus four insurance policies collected over the years. Your job, as financial advisor, is to take all the data, organize it, make observations, recommend strategies and wrap it all up for the Coles in a way that compels them to take action. This is, and has always been, one of the cornerstones of your job.

Now, rewind: I would like you to take that box of statements and place it on the lap of a ParaPlanner.

I know, it's shocking! You're saying to yourself, "But Lauren! I can't do that! Sure, it can be tedious, but I need to do the financial analysis for the Coles! How will I even know what I'm talking about if I don't work through the numbers myself?" Maybe you actually enjoy the number crunching. Maybe you love the design aspect of the task, the feeling of solving a technical puzzle, of fitting the pieces together and crafting a well-thought out plan. It's natural to feel that way. If you do, it's probably because you've got the single piece of DNA most required for the ParaPlanner, **the Analytical Gene**. All I'm saying is, let's find someone else with the gene and let him or her take a crack at it.

Who's got the gene? We want Nate Powell. Nate is a guy I know who loves numbers. When he was a kid, he'd buy a little pencil and box scorecard whenever he went to a baseball game, so he could record every at bat. And to this day, he still does. He also loves systems and statistics. He can talk for hours about his weekend in Las Vegas, how he lost a huge hand of Texas Hold'em because some dummy chased a gut-shot straight draw with only a 13% chance of catching it, then beat him on the river. Now I can barely understand what Nate is explaining to me when he talks about this stuff, but I do understand that he has that wonderful number-crunching analytical gene.

The fact is that many financial advisors come into the business expressly to perform the technical work of financial planning and, with horror, discover the well-kept secret about the industry. The secret is, you can have the finest financial mind in the world, but you won't be able to use it until clients are in front of you. If you're able to prospect and to cultivate relationships, and you're reading this book, you're going to be successful. But if you're a financial advisor who wants to perform analytical work exclusively, you'll starve. In fact, our industry is riddled with failed advisors who entered the business with one expectation and realized another. Your ParaPlanner may be recruited from these ranks.

And although a failed advisor may make an extraordinarily successful ParaPlanner (essentially, an inside planner), there are other places to look for someone with the analytical gene...from your accountant, to the guy sitting next to you on a plane, solving his book of "Sudoku" puzzles. It's the problem solving aspect we're looking for here, someone who can take disparate data points, synthesize them into strategies to create solutions. Analytical types tend to enjoy working on projects quietly and often retreat to their desks for a few hours, not returning to the world until the dots in the their well-crafted financial plans are connected perfectly.

The Job

Where does the ParaPlanner fit into your practice? At the most basic entry level, the ParaPlanner is capable of taking data from a source document and getting it in the right box in your planning software. If they can easily do their own taxes or are skilled at balancing a checking account, they've got a head start at this job. But if the ParaPlanner is smart, the role should quickly grow. The ParaPlanner should receive the same technical training as an advisor in your company would and should also be the liaison with the wholesalers with whom you work. Understanding products, process and planning strategies is essential in this role.

A good ParaPlanner should be able to sit down with you after your first client meeting, debrief, and help you prepare for the data meeting.

This includes designing the agenda for the next meeting. When the data meeting occurs, the ParaPlanner should be able to take that data, enter it into your software and develop a plan. When you take that plan to the implementation phase, the ParaPlanner will be right there to support you. And once the plan is implemented, the ParaPlanner will most definitely help you monitor investment accounts and insurance policies. The more you trust in your ParaPlanner, the faster they will develop.

And what a pleasure it is when they do. Imagine having someone on your staff capable of handling comprehensive financial planning. Someone skilled at estate plan design. Someone who knows your investment planning tools backwards and forwards, someone knowledgeable with Efficient Frontier, Monte Carlo Simulation, and Morningstar research. Someone who can create investment reviews, craft performance reports, perform insurance policy audits and prepare insurance illustrations. Someone who can take a massive, time-consuming aspect of your job, and do it for you as well as you can do it yourself – and perhaps better. This is the ParaPlanner.

And it doesn't end there. ParaPlanners tend to be on the "techie" side, and for that reason can provide great technology support. They are generally early adaptors of technology and will lead the charge in introducing new planning and practice management technology tools to the practice.

At the highest levels, we see several important variations on the ParaPlanner role. Practices that reach a certain size will often develop senior ParaPlanners into *Case Managers*, dedicated to the design and manufacture of financial plans. Some become *Directors of Planning*, overseeing a team of ParaPlanners serving underneath them. Another effective variation on the role is a *Director of Investments*; someone who develops investment plans, selects platforms and managers, and oversees a team that monitors, implements and supports client investment strategies.

Conclusion

There is no doubt the ParaPlanner role offers an exciting staffing dimension. But the real decision lies with you. Sure, it's easy to hire an Administrative Assistant...you hate the paperwork and would love to delegate it. The question is, will you delegate tasks you may enjoy? Tasks that, for some of you, have been fundamental and mandatory components of your job? I think you will. Because you know that every task you delegate effectively means more time for you to do what you love...be in front of clients helping them make momentous decisions in their lives.

The Concierge

All of the four support positions on our *"Dream Team"* staffing model are designed to improve your bottom line by leveraging your time and energy. But only one role is designed to improve your *top line*... by nurturing and growing client relationships. Now, if I told you there were four potential roles to add to your company, and only one of the four could immediately make you more money, you'd hire that one, right? Well as obvious a decision as it might seem, most advisors are in such a hurry to stop doing paperwork they run out and hire an Administrative Assistant without even thinking about this other role. In fact, the lion's share of planners may not realize this role exists. So with that in mind, let me introduce you to the third member of our Dream Team, **The Concierge**.

The Concierge has a number of responsibilities, but in essence this person does just two things. They help you find and keep clients. Since "finding and keeping clients" is the definition of marketing, many of you may refer to this person as your Marketing Specialist. Whether you call them a Marketing Specialist or use the more client-centric term of "Concierge," these people nurture the essential relationships of your business – the ones you have with prospects, clients, attorneys, CPA's and other centers of influence. This person works every day to find new clients, get them in the door, and turn them into raving fans. They do this primarily with one gene, one piece of DNA that's easy to spot and impossible to fake.

The Gene

Since Alexander Graham Bell introduced the first telephone, teenagers have abused it. While it is difficult for parents to understand the hours of time that can be devoted to the discussion of lip-gloss or whether he likes her or *likes her, likes her*, the chatting sorority continues to flourish. Some of these marvelous young girls, and sometimes very social young men, take their chatting beyond the realm of hobby, elevating it to art form...their mastery of the medium almost classifies as a separate language. My daughter, JoJo, was one such girl. Somehow, by uttering "Oh my gosh!" "No Way!" and "Like, totally!" for several hours a day, she was able to accomplish minor organizational feats: organize fifty apathetic freshmen to design a homecoming float, keep tabs on every single boy at school, or successfully play matchmaker with the junior varsity quarterback and the head cheerleader. Now, having a chatty butterfly of a daughter can be a headache for parents, but darned if they don't turn out to be prime candidates for our Concierge position. And their qualification is, quite simply, **the Social Gene.**

You don't need to look for any little clues as to the presence of the social gene. It's obvious who has it and who doesn't. Whereas we might notice a paper-fondler and quietly comment to ourselves, "Oh, he's got the organization gene," or spy someone managing their fantasy football team and immediately catch a whiff of their analytical DNA, it takes no such level of detective work to isolate the social people. They're the ones smiling, shaking hands, sometimes hugging, asking you about your day or your job or your life. They're calling you on the phone or paying you a visit, often to sell you something, because that's one thing they're pretty good at. But whether they're selling or schmoozing or just saying hi, individuals with the social gene do one thing very, very well -- establish rapport. It's lesson number one in sales and our social butterflies don't need to be taught it. Making people feel comfortable, on the phone or in person, is just second nature to any truly social person. Now, some of you are quite gifted in this area yourselves, others average, and some downright mediocre. But no matter where you fall on the social spectrum, adding a Concierge to your practice will pay immediate dividends.

The Job

The first responsibility you will pass on to your Concierge is managing the prospect pipeline. This is where there is immediate progress to be made in almost every practice. Why? Because most advisors, even the most talented networkers, are notoriously bad at following up with referrals. They may have a system to garner referrals, they may have fifty prospects waiting to be contacted, but they procrastinate.

When they finally get around to thinking about calling, they convince themselves that the introduction is now cold. And they're probably right. So the first thing the Concierge will focus on is getting prospect information into the data base and assuring an appointment is made. Most advisors believe in setting this first appointment themselves – and your Concierge will stay on top of the referral and you, assuring this essential call is made. Some advisors will delegate this task and have the Concierge make the call...after all, to this person there's almost no such thing as a cold call.

Perhaps the most important duty you'll pass on to the Concierge is developing and implementing your annual marketing plan. This plan will no doubt include measurable goals for referrals, annual reviews, strategic alliance cultivation and client touches such as newsletters, monthly calls, holiday gifts and other scheduled communications. You probably already do many of these with one minor hitch...the word "scheduled" isn't part of the equation. Most advisors will pick up the phone, off the cuff, when they feel they owe a client a call. With the help of a Concierge and a little technology, such touches become standardized.

Vital to any marketing strategy are client appreciation events. Again, most advisors have a bag of tricks they rely on for such events, ranging from golf tournaments to educational seminars. With a Concierge, you can hand off not only the planning and coordination of these events, but also the conceptual process. A good Concierge loves nothing better than to think of fun, constructive ways to get clients together, plus a few of their advisorless friends, and schmooze them like a pro once she's in front of them. From private chef's dinners, to the VIP box at the ball game, to wine tasting, to private premiers of new shows, the Concierge delights in coming up with a constant stream of new ways to keep clients engaged and referrals coming.

And when it comes to referrals, the Concierge will also foster relationships beyond current and prospective clients. An important of their job is to nurture *Center of Influence* relationships. These are the attorneys, the CPAs and the property and casualty brokers with whom you work...people who are in a prime position to *possibly* refer you business. The extent to which they *actually* refer business to you depends entirely on how well you take care of them. Obviously, they are looking for the same thing from you that you want from them – introductions. But your Concierge can help glue those Centers of Influence to the practice in the same way she glues your clients – by touching them frequently and making them feel important.

As I mentioned before, people with the social gene tend to be great sales people, for obvious reasons. Now they may only be using their sales skills indirectly in the Concierge role, but a good advisor will make use of their Concierge's sales talents. In fact, one of the finest uses of this role is as a personal sales coach. To some extent this is completely voluntary. A lot of people in this role will naturally ask, "So, did you get 'em?" as you stroll back into the office after a client meeting. But, if encouraged, a good Concierge will not only know what prospects are in the pipeline and which need to be called by you, they'll also hold you to task when it comes to closing them.

Things You Can't Teach

Your Concierge is on a phone call with your one of your biggest clients, The Kennedys, checking to see if they've signed the forms you sent over. Before even talking to Mrs. Kennedy about the signature, the Concierge naturally starts chatting with her about life and her husband, and learns that the Kennedy's 25th Anniversary is coming up. When she hears they'll be spending the anniversary in Paris, the Concierge just gushes...she spent a semester there during college and could talk about Paris for hours. When the call is over, the Concierge walks into your office and says "The Kennedy's will be staying at the George V Hotel in Paris for their anniversary. Shall we have a bottle of champagne waiting for them with your compliments?" This Concierge is effective in a variety of ways. Not just for thinking to send a gift (which you might not have), or for actually taking the time to make arrangements and have the champagne delivered (which you probably would not have). No, the true gift of this Concierge is her ability to establish intimacy...to get a client to discuss anniversary and travel plans on what would otherwise have been a thirty second phone call. As opposed to your ParaPlanner, who may get nervous on the phone ordering Chinese food, the Concierge's bread and butter is seeing the potential in each and every client exchange.

Conclusion

Of the four positions on The Dream Team, The Concierge role is, without a doubt, the least employed, a fact that frustrates me to no end. Advisors should be jumping on this. This person *will* make you money. Twenty years from now, I believe this position will be far more prolific in our industry, but right now the field is wide open and you'll be way ahead of the pack if you add this role now. And while it may seem like a luxury position, one afforded only by advisors with big client lists and incomes, the opposite is also true. I think one of the best times to hire a Concierge is when you're relatively new to the business. When I meet with an advisor who is just starting out and needs more business, I frequently suggest postponing the Administrative Assistant hire in favor of acquiring a Concierge, or perhaps hiring both in a part-time capacity (we'll return to this concept soon). Remember: as much as you might hate paperwork, you may want to consider toughing it out and adding a component to your practice that actually improves your top line. If the business is growing, you'll be able to afford more staff anyway.

In fact, I believe both your client list and staff will expand to the point where you need one final addition to your practice, one role that will optimize all the roles we've discussed. Someone to captain and complete your Dream Team. And wouldn't you know? I've got the perfect person in mind.

The Practice Manager

I believe that practice management is like a stage performance. There are actors, scripts and props. Every day brings a new, live audience. A director pulls these disparate elements together to create a memorable performance night after night. There are many practices with employees who are fine actors and some practices that do quite well with their scripts or processes. But, in almost all cases, the Advisor/Owner ends up being both lead actor AND director. And, with all do respect to the amazing advisors to whom I've dedicated my career; the vast majority are far better at acting than directing!

So who can free the advisor to focus exclusively on his or her performance and deliver a great audience experience? It's the **Practice Manager**. This role, also known as Director of Operations, is new to our industry. I can count the number of these positions in the country but almost every client of mine gets one. Because the moment the Practice Manager takes over managing operations, staffing, and projects is the moment the advisor is finally free to do what he or she loves.

The Genes

At the age of four I had a friend, Wendy. Wendy was an outgoing little girl, kind of bossy, and an obvious organizer. If we were playing house, she was the one who decided who was the mom and who was the dad and who was the baby, then assigned everybody his or her household chores. At seven, I met her male counterpart, Matt – he was the kid who always decided if the game that day would be basketball or four square or kickball, then send somebody to grab the equipment while he nominated captains and started picking teams. I lost touch with both Wendy and Matt over the years but wherever they are today, I wish two things for them: One is that they're not married to each other, because they'd drive each other crazy. The other is that they became Practice Managers.

Wendy and Matt had the **Take-Charge Gene**. And while a lot of people have strong interpersonal skills, or just like to be the boss, that doesn't necessarily mean they have the take-charge gene. What we're looking for more than anything else is someone who gets things done. And, if they get them done by orchestrating the efforts of others, they are a natural manager.

The simplest way to distinguish a manager from a non-manger is this: when given a task, is the person more likely to delegate it, or do it themselves? A manager would always prefer to delegate it. You probably won't be surprised to learn that Wendy was in charge of planning my high school prom. I can still see her pointing out where to hang the streamers and what songs to play and determining how to man the ticket table. In fact, I remember one fellow prom planner, Kay, complaining about her as we set up: "She just tells everybody what to do. If I were she, I'd be hanging twice as many streamers as everyone else to set an example." Kay was right…she was a workaholic, and the kind of person who would rather do something herself than spend precious time trying to get somebody else to do it. Now, maybe Wendy didn't hang a single streamer, play a single song, or punch a single ticket. But the prom went off splendidly. And if Kay had been in charge, she herself might have hung streamers well into the night, but without the efforts of a larger team we might not have had a prom at all.

So first, a good manager is a *good delegator*. A lot of people have trouble delegating. Perhaps a task seems too small and insignificant to delegate, so they figure it would be easier to do themselves. The opposite is also common; with people frequently thinking a project is too big or too important to be left to anyone but themselves. Of course, the slippery slope is obvious…eventually pretty much everything starts to fall into the "too big to delegate" or "too small to delegate" category, and you're doing everything yourself. Good managers are adept at shifting work to others, and are effective at knowing to whom to delegate.

Second, managers have excellent *communication skills*. Once a task is delegated, they can explain the project dimensions clearly and effectively. They don't drop a project on someone's desk and say, "Have this done by Friday." They make sure the task requirements have been conveyed, so that the task won't come back a day late or a dollar short.

Third, we need someone who understands how to *motivate* those to whom they delegate. Poor motivators make poor managers, because no matter how much delegating and communicating is done, positive results are achieved only when the people doing the job feel that there's something in it for them. Different people are motivated by different things and great managers are adept at knowing what flavor carrots to use.

And last, we need someone strong enough to control the action. Someone who, once a task is assigned, will not be shy about making sure the work gets done.

So that's the DNA of a Practice Manager. Who needs one? Most every practice with three of more employees and certainly any producer group that shares core staff. At what point is the addition of this position financially viable? Probably when gross revenues exceed $1,000,000. When is the right time to start thinking about this position? Probably right now. I want you to really get a feel for this role, whether you add it to your team tomorrow or ten years from now.

The Job

The Practice Manager manages. This much is obvious. If you have in your employ an Administrative Assistant, a ParaPlanner, and a Concierge, the addition of a Practice Manager will bring management oversight to the team. For instance, let's say you have a project that requires a team effort—converting to a paperless office, maybe. Even if you've got an outstanding person in your ParaPlanner role, they can only be accountable for their share of the project. And often times where the ParaPlanner's duties end and the Administrative Assistant's begin is a gray area. A Practice Manager brings clarity and accountability. Ultimately it is the Practice Manager's job to make sure the project is completed, and you'll be going to them if it is not.

Operations Leadership

But the Practice Manager is about much more than just performance monitoring or task management. If they're great, they will model the behavior that all other team members will emulate. They'll help those team members grow professionally. They'll come up with systems for marketing, planning, implementation, service and practice management and they'll assure those systems are captured in procedures manuals. They'll make sure that all functions are cross-trained. They'll hire, they'll train, and they'll manage office moves and new technology projects. Most important, they'll take your actors, your scripts and your props and they will pull them together, night after night, to deliver an amazing performance for the lucky people in your audience.

A "roll up the sleeves" style

My son worked for several years at a small restaurant, which functioned just like many of the practices I have seen. In a big restaurant, a server or bartender can call in sick, and there is usually enough staff to cover for them without interruption of service. But if you've only got one bartender and they can't come in, what do you do? A manager at a small restaurant must be able to do every job, from taking orders to mixing drinks to bussing tables. They needn't be terrific at each duty, but they must be able to perform it in a crunch. So too must the Practice Manager be a utility player on your team, capable of stepping in to any role when needed.

An appreciation for technology

And when it comes to innovation, the Practice Manager should be your team's brightest star. Managers are, by nature, inclined to systems and processes. I can say this from personal experience. I remember when I was growing up in Teaneck, New Jersey, making myself a bowl of cereal, and counting the steps from the cupboard to the refrigerator to the table and wondering if there was a quicker way to do it! So too will your Practice Manager have similar inklings. A good Practice Manager may only have been working for you for one week, and already is saying "We've got client data in Outlook, in Excel, and in paper files...we should have all this data in one place!" And while the Practice Manager isn't necessarily a techie who can write code or design programs, they should be curious about technology. They may not know how to write a complex macro in Excel but they know when one should be written and they find the person who can do it.

An inclination toward systems

Systems improvements certainly aren't confined to technology. Your Practice Manager might see the way you handle new VIP clients, and say, "Shouldn't we have a system for this?" When big clients are coming in, the Practice Manager might send an "excitement email" to all the staff. Have the Administrative Assistant ready with the client's beverage of choice, which the Concierge has on file, because the Practice Manager created a system for it. Are you having their car washed during the meeting? No more running around five minutes before they get to the office to figure these things out. The Practice Manager should not only be on top of it, they have created a system so that it runs smoothly every time.

Staffing Strength

But of all these duties, the most important responsibility performed by the Practice Manager is staff management. Especially given the frequency of turnover in our industry, this is truly an area where I love to see advisors relinquishing control and handing it over to somebody who can do it faster, better and cheaper. A common example is your assistant gets pregnant, and decides to take two years off work. How many hours will it take you to replace her? Don't just think about posting an ad on an internet job board and going through resumes. Think about the entire process: interviews, testing, reference checks, offer letters, orientation, and training. I'd say for most advisors that this process takes about 100 hours, which is pretty conservative, and that's assuming you hired someone who sticks. So, depending on your hourly rate (net revenue/2,080) the hiring process, calculated hourly, could easily cost you $25,000 to $75,000. You will reduce this number dramatically and achieve better results by delegating the hiring to your Practice Manager. If hiring were rare in our industry I could see glossing over this duty, but in reality the opposite is quite true…we do tons of hiring. This is especially true of group practices, which typically employ more people and have additional roles for compliance, office support, technology and business processing. In those producer group practices, a Practice Manager is almost always a necessity.

Conclusion

All these duties add up to one basic, over-arching responsibility: the Practice Manager runs the practice. Between managing client projects and managing staff, what the Practice Manager brings to the advisor is simplicity. You don't need to interact so much with everyone on the team. Rather, you deal primarily with someone you know, like, and trust. And once a task is delegated to them, you don't have to follow up. The rest of the staff will now report through the Practice Manager, and it is the Practice Manager who will be responsible for task management, hiring and performance monitoring. Moreover, the Practice Manager knows how the staff is doing, how they're feeling and how best to deploy their talents. This is real freedom for the advisor and, in my opinion, is the holy grail of staffing for every successful, high-end practice.

The Associate Advisor

So you've built a nice little Dream Team. It started small, perhaps with an Administrative Assistant or Concierge when your business was new, and soon you added a ParaPlanner to help with planning and investment design. When your staff got large enough you even recruited a Practice Manager to run the show. And, if you're not concerned with building a practice that will continue after you're gone, you may continue staffing your business exclusively with these employees and will probably do just fine.

But if you envision turning over the reins to a person or persons whom you have personally groomed, with whom your clients are familiar and comfortable, and who will one day be in a position to buy you out, then one final Dream Team role is required. I am speaking of a Junior Advisor.

The Junior Advisor role, which I'll refer to as **Associate Advisor**, since nobody likes to be a *junior* anything, is unique on the Dream Team for several reasons. One reason is that this is the only role we will not discuss in the recruitment section of the book. That is because, more than any other role, I believe this person is best grown organically, rather than hired from the outside. Another reason it is unique is that before you create this role within your practice, you must first go through some serious introspection. You must ask yourself some tough questions: "Do I really want to share my business?" "Do I know what role I want to play in a partnership?" "Do I know what roles need to be played by others?" "Will I enjoy mentoring a junior?" "Will I be able to relinquish control?"

When the time comes that you answer these questions in the affirmative, you will be ready to explore the many benefits of an Associate Advisor.

The Genes

For the previous Dream team positions we've discussed, I gave you examples of the specific genes that are required to do the job. But for your Associate Advisor, this discussion is a little different.

The genes that make a good Associate Advisor are genes that make a good, well...*you*. And that can be a lot of things. Creating and sustaining a successful business can be achieved through a variety of genes. What makes Steve Jobs successful is not necessarily what makes Warren Buffet successful. Advisors are the same way; they come in all shapes and sizes. Some are incredible marketers, others fantastic at process. Some make it on sheer determination.

What we do know is that there are two genes that you *definitely* have, and that if your Associate Advisor is missing them he or she will be in for an uphill battle. These are the **Rainmaking Gene** and the **Relationship-Building Gene**. The first drives your ability to bring in new business...the extent to which you can create new client opportunities dictates your success early on in our industry, and the same will be true of your successor. If they can't bring in new clients, your practice will not be long for this world after you transition out.

Relationship building is equally important, because once you find new clients you have to nurture and grow them. In this area it is important that your Associate Advisor have a bedside manner similar to your own. He or she will need to replicate the talents that have glued your clients to *you*.

So the must-have genes in your Associate Advisor are the ability to hunt for new clients and the talent to fulfill the needs of your existing ones. In practice, this point is frequently overlooked as the Senior Advisor may be more focused on the technical expertise of his or her junior. This approach is understandable, but shortsighted.

Sharing values and some key character traits with your junior is critical. But magic will happen when the Associate Advisor layers on his or her strengths in other areas. Beyond these two genes, your Associate

Advisor might be a genius at investment design or estate planning. Maybe they're a marketing whiz. Your practice needs will dictate how crucial these secondary strengths are. And where do we find people with these traits, be they analytical or social? You guessed it - look no further than the ranks of your own ParaPlanner or Concierge for these abilities. These people have already inculcated your brand, understand you and have strong relationships with other team members. We will discuss this in greater detail later, when we learn about *Career Paths*. But for now, let's focus on how we groom our Associate Advisors and what they provide both you and your clients.

Grooming an Associate Advisor

When it comes to training and molding an Associate Advisor there seems to be two schools of thought. And these two schools mirror closely the styles of the advisors who promote their use. The first school of thought says that nobody should be in front of a client who hasn't moved up through the ranks and learned all the ins and outs of planning strategies, processes, products, and operations. Advisors who subscribe to this school of thought generally won't put an Associate Advisor in front of a client until they've earned their stripes through a backroom apprenticeship of two or more years in duration.

The second camp believes an associate should go into production after a modicum of training, citing that the most important parts of the business—identifying prospects, closing and relationship building—can't be learned in the backroom.

Now, I'm not going to convince you that one school of thought is better than the other, because in reality I believe both have pros and cons, and that the approach you take has everything to do with your personal beliefs. I will say that if I were bringing one of my kids into this industry, I would probably want them to know the business from the inside out. However, I would be bringing them into client meetings very early on, with an eye on developing their professional poise simultaneously with developing their knowledge of products and process. In addition I'd probably want them to get comfortable setting appointments with clients and conducting review meetings where client needs were fairly basic. So, in essence, I believe a hybrid approach between backroom and front room yields the best results.

One of the things that advisors struggle with is positioning their Associate Advisor with a client. They fear that the client will inevitably think, and possibly ask, "Why is this person here when they've never been here before?" In dealing with this question, our goal becomes how to describe this new role in a way that makes both Associate and client feel good. Where I've seen the most successful senior/junior relationships, the senior introduces the junior as a partner, period. Doing so does not necessarily imply an equal partnership or equal roles, but it does imply that the associate has a vested interest in the client's wellbeing.

When introducing your associate, avoid language or phrases that de-position. Saying to your client, "This is John. He's here to take notes," is a good way to make John feel like a secretary and assure that the client will *never* call John with any technical needs. I suggest something more like this: "I'd like you to meet my partner, John. John is a CFP®, he's got an MBA from Georgetown, and he's the best person I know at getting financial plans implemented." Create a positive foundation, and both client and associate will follow your lead.

Any form of a partnership carries with it the likelihood of unmet expectations. So setting expectations with regard to roles, job duties, activity, communication and production is essential. If you hired the right Associate Advisor and he or she failed, it was probably because there was little accountability and little coaching. When you bring a junior into your practice you must be prepared to assume the role of Sales Manager. If this is a hat you don't enjoy wearing, then bringing in a junior is likely going to be a costly and draining failed experiment.

The Job

There are many reasons advisors look to add juniors but, essentially, they fall into five buckets.

Reason #1: To provide a built-in practice succession plan. A lot of advisors believe the "Succession Fairy" is going to visit them and write them a big fat check at the moment they decide they don't want to do this stuff anymore. This *might* happen. But the way to assure that it does is by building recurring revenue sources, having a professional support team and being a process and data-driven practice. You'll spend years, perhaps decades, cultivating strong client relationships. The right Associate Advisor will ensure that the revenue streams behind those clients continue to grow after you are gone and that the clients you love continue to be served in the manner to which to which they've become accustomed.

Reason #2: To take day-to-day service responsibilities off your shoulders. An Associate can be expected to develop financial and investment plans, handle implementation for your 'A' clients, handle service issues for your 'B' and 'C' clients, and conduct reviews with 'B' and 'C' clients. The earlier you are able to get your Associate in front of clients, the sooner these clients will be able to pick up the phone and talk to someone other than you about service issues. If your Associate is informed, savvy, and ready to help, clients will soon feel comfortable going directly to him or her and that translates to more free time for you.

Reason #3: To bring business into the practice. Let's face it. Just because you have sustained a practice for years doesn't mean you're a rainmaker. There are many brilliant advisors who suffer from call reluctance, who use no referral systems and would sooner have a root canal than ask someone for their business. They see a junior as a means to bring business in the door.

Reason #4: Synergy. You're a genius with estate planning but you leave millions of investment dollars on the table. Or the reverse – you design amazing investment portfolios but you're allergic to life insurance. An Associate Advisor can fill a critical void in your practice lineup – perhaps being the first step toward becoming a true wealth management firm.

All of these are darn good reasons to recruit an Associate Advisor. But the most important reason is our last:

Reason #5: For your clients. We're in the peace of mind business, the risk management and mitigation business, and the financial security business. And yet, so many advisors fail to plan for the day they are no longer there to serve their clients. Clients want to know that, when that day comes – and it will – there will be people who know them, care about them, and who will seamlessly step in to continue the work that you began.

Conclusion

Grooming an Associate Advisor takes careful selection, years of work, and a good deal of patience. But the payoffs are huge and you don't have to wait for your curtain call to enjoy them. Your Associate Advisor will lighten your service load, add technical depth to your practice and help you manage and grow your business. And at the end of the day, the true peace of mind gained will be yours…knowing that the business you created will go on after you retire. Our business is about helping people plan, helping them make sure that what they do today will count for something tomorrow. With an Associate Advisor, you've demonstrated that you've put your own house in order – just as you help your clients to do.

The Hire

Develop A Job Description

Congratulations! You've learned the five roles which comprise *The Dream Team*, and have a good idea of who you need to hire first. It wasn't easy…you had to read a bunch of pages in a book and listen to me ramble about people you've never met. So I'm throwing confetti on you and blowing my kazoo and playing "Celebration" by *Kool and the Gang*. I'm proud of you! And you're clapping your hands and saying, "Yeah, Lauren! Now that I know who I want, it's time to go interview people and hire them!"

Whoah! Stop the music. Someone sweep up the confetti. And pass those kazoos up to the front. Because right here, on the road to a great hire, is the step most advisors skip. It's the 'aim' in "ready, aim, fire." It's the **job description**. Now if you've ever worked in the corporate world you probably feel that there's nothing more irrelevant than a job description. But I'm going to show you how to create high impact job descriptions that will pay you back again and again. In fact, this single tool *facilitates* so much else that I consider it to be the Swiss Army Knife of practice management. Why?

It forces you to think before you hire.

Most advisors staff reactively: "I'm dying of paperwork. I need to hire someone." Yup, you do. But what will be the overall purpose for the role you add? What will the specific responsibilities within this role be? What are your expectations for how these responsibilities will be performed? And most importantly, what talents are needed to shine in this particular role? Investing an hour in writing a job description using the template I'm going to provide is the equivalent of writing a business plan for the position you're about to add. It defines purpose, tactics and performance measures. And it paints a vivid picture of your ideal hire.

It makes many other tasks easier.

With your job description complete, crafting a job posting is a snap. Showing a candidate what the job entails – effortless. Giving a new employee their marching orders on day one – done. I'm even going to show you how to turn a job description into a training outline. All these challenges will be easy hurdles for you because you invested an hour in creating clarity – for yourself and the wonderful person who's about to free you from backroom frustration.

It creates a shared understanding of what the job is.

The biggest difference between a useless job description and what *you* are going to create is the addition of something called "deliverables." Deliverables are performance measures that spell out how quickly, how frequently or how accurately a responsibility is carried out. This is the step that allows you to set the par for the hole. And when you and your employee know what par is, you both have a much better shot at achieving it. A well-crafted job description can become a coaching anchor for you, the basis from which you can reward incredible performance as well as get lack-luster performance back on track.

It tells you "who's on first."

As your practice grows, so will your staff. And as soon as you have more than one person supporting you, the chance for role ambiguity is likely. A very common form of practice dysfunction occurs when there is a pattern of multiple people inadvertently performing the same tasks. This typically occurs when roles are not clearly communicated. And what's the best way to communicate the role? You guessed it. The job description.

As you can see, the benefits are evident. Now, let me show you the three-step process for creating your own powerful job descriptions.

Step 1: Identify the broad components of the job

The first thing we want to do is simply nail down the big-picture components of the job. Let's say you're hiring your first Administrative Assistant...the classic "everything" person. The broad components of this job are probably:

- Administrative support

- Business processing

- Client service

- Marketing support

- Technology

- Compliance

Step 2: Identify the responsibilities within each component

For each of the broad components above, identify key responsibilities that fall under them. For instance, the category of "Client Service" might include:

"Respond to in-bound requests for service"

"Capture all service requests in data base history"

In this step, I have two pieces of advice. The first: Don't get bogged down in minutia. Group like tasks under one responsibility, where possible. That being said, you don't want to leave out any tasks that aren't explicitly covered by another category. Which brings me to my second piece of advice: Don't sugarcoat the job description. If you don't tell someone they're in charge of watering the plants, you'll be left hoping they do it, watering them yourself, or most likely, working next to a dead plant.

Step 3: Identify a performance measure or benchmark for each responsibility

This third and final step is by far the most important and is what will elevate your job description from the typical useless piece of paper to an accountability anchor in your practice.

A performance measure or benchmark is simply a way for you to say how quickly, completely, accurately or consistently a task should be performed. This is where most job descriptions are sorely lacking. Most advisors would include answering phones as a responsibility under "Administrative Support" but that's where they stop. To me, "answering phones" is not a job description. A monkey can pick up a ringing phone. I want my assistant to answer calls within three rings, with a smile on her face. That's my performance benchmark. And I put it right down on paper; so that when I hire that assistant there will be no misunderstanding about what great performance looks like. When it comes to reception, my assistant's job is not to answer phones. Her job is to answer the phone within three rings with a smile on her face.

Note: If you're imagining me, lurking behind my assistant like a vulture, ready to scream "Ha! That was four rings! You're fired!", please think again. In any busy office service standards will occasionally slip. This is unavoidable. So long as your benchmark is reasonable, it's better to have the mark be missed once in a while than to simply have no standard at all. And while you may think that specific performance measures for something as basic as answering the phone is too nit-picky, I'd urge you to think again—this is how we begin to build accountability at every level. Being specific and deliberate with your expectations will get you the systemic practice consistency you crave!

So when we combine our broad categories, the individual responsibilities, and the deliverable we expect for each responsibility, we achieve a comprehensive job description. A sample job description using this approach can be found on my website, http://www.giftedpractice.com. To download this and all other templates referenced in this book, go to the Resource page of the website and enter the password, *mystafftolast.*

So, when you're ready to jump into recruiting, put the brakes on just long enough to develop a meaningful job description using the Category/Responsibility/Deliverable template. With a strong job description in hand, you'll have the bait you need to attract top-tier applicants.

Now you just need to learn where to cast your line.

Advertise Your Job Opening

Getting the word out about a job opening is easy, and it's about to get easier. We can thank the Internet in large part for this. It has never been so simple to reach so many, and at such a small cost. And while advertising a job opening on career websites will be a fruitful medium for most readers, I want to take some time first to point out that while it may be a *good* way to find applicants, it certainly is not the *only* way, and there's no reason why you should limit your fishing to just one choice spot. So where do we find prospective employees?

On the Street

Remember all the time we spent talking about the "genes" that make somebody great at each Dream Team position? Well, one great by-product of learning those traits is that you are now a qualified talent scout, inside and outside your firm. Who knows…your next Administrative Assistant might be that sweet, detail-oriented loan processor you met while refinancing your mortgage. Your next Concierge may be your Pastor's wife, who knows everyone in the congregation and plans every church event with charm and ease. Marilyn Monroe was discovered by a photographer sent out to take pictures of pretty girls helping with the war effort in 1945, and was soon on her way to modeling and movie stardom. You too are now capable of "discovering" someone with the talents your practice needs. Does that waitress have the "it" factor you need? Nobody knows better than you.

There's one place that personal observation recruiting may take you but that I do *not* recommend as a recruiting resource. It's your gym. After many failed attempts at hiring the cute and lively young women who frequently work at the front desk of health clubs, I have come to call this recruiting opportunity "Gym Nauseum." What I've found is that that front desk person typically doesn't have office experience, doesn't love paperwork and likes a job where she can move around freely and interact with customers. Maybe you could convince me that she'd make a great Concierge, but you're taking a risk with that friendly gal behind the desk at Bally's.

Ask your Clients

If you want to find someone who will best serve your clients, why not ask your clients themselves? They have an intimate understanding of what you and the members of your team do. You don't have to send out an all points bulletin saying "SOS, I'm losing my right hand, who do you know?" But you can ask select clients. In fact, one of your very own clients may want the job – I can't tell you how many clients we've hired to work for their very own advisors. If that isn't a testimonial, I don't know what is!

If you are considering hiring a client or a family member, consider them ONLY if they are tailor-made for the position and have a successful track record. Undoing a mis-hire is difficult. Undoing a mis-hire involving a client, child of a client, or relative is worse. Much worse.

Non-Web Advertising

Print advertisements may be a dying breed, but they're not dead yet. And depending on where you practice, they might be a valuable resource. While, in general, advertising in a local paper is more expensive and reaches fewer people than web-based marketing, there are circumstances where it makes sense. If the position is part-time, and if the job is relatively administrative or clerical, and if the community is small, you may want to put an old-fashioned help-wanted add in the local paper. If you work in Ponte Verde Beach, Florida, a lot of your potential applicants probably read the local paper more than they surf the big career websites. Yet if you're seeking a non-administrative position…say a ParaPlanner as opposed to an assistant…I'd be inclined to use the web. Remember, you get whom you advertise to. I don't mind hiring a receptionist who is more comfortable searching for jobs in a newspaper than a website, but I'd expect a ParaPlanner to use a more modern approach to seeking employment.

Non-web advertising isn't limited to print media. Get creative with your job promotion. Do you have a church or synagogue bulletin board or newsletter? How about regional conferences, like FPA and NAIFA meetings? Get the word out wherever you are, if you think the kind of person you're looking for might be around. If you love your current staff, ask for their help as well. You can even offer a $500 bonus if they refer someone who becomes a long-term employee. Remember, we're just looking for as many quality applicants as we can find.

The World Wide Web

Last, and absolutely not least, are online employment websites. There are scores of employment websites – the big, general ones like *Monster, CareerBuilder* and *Hotjobs* and scores of industry specific ones like *WallStreetJobs*. The organizations that represent us like MDRT, FPA, and the Society for Financial Services Professionals, all have career sections on their sites, where, for a modest amount of money, you can advertise your opening. For my clients, I use *Careerbuilder* and/or *Monster* and because Craigslist is either free or ridiculously inexpensive, I almost always post there as well. *Careerbuilder, Monster* and *Hotjobs* all provide some nice organizational tools to help you manage your recruiting process, organize résumés and respond to candidates.

Writing your Job Post

The purpose of the job post is to attract as many qualified candidates as possible. The way to attract candidates is to paint the picture of what a successful candidate looks like and then describe the position in an accurate but compelling way. I want candidates to read my posts and say, "That's me! They're looking for me!" So a job post I write for an Administrative Assistant might sound something like this:

> *"You're an administrative pro who doesn't want to be a secretary. You have top notch Microsoft Office skills. You love organizing paper and projects. You're a pit bull when it comes to follow through and details*

> *rarely slip through your grasp. You enjoy filling out forms thoroughly and accurately."*

That's how *I* find an organized person. Anybody who thinks that sounds like them is a good candidate. And if an applicant reads that and doesn't fit the bill, they'll know it and generally won't respond, which is good. Web posting is going to get you a ton of responses, probably more than you can handle, and it's smart to thin out the herd with specific requirements in your post.

You can download a sample job post for an Administrative Assistant from my website and use as-is or as a template for other positions. As you craft your job post, focus on describing the skills, behaviors and credentials of the person you're seeking rather than every minute job responsibility.

If you employ a range of recruiting resources you will, no doubt, create a large pool of applicants from which to choose a new team member. It might be a *very* large pool that we're going to trim down. The important thing is that somewhere in that pile of resumes is the newest member of your staff, just waiting to be offered the opportunity.

And so we come to what may be the most pivotal part of the staffing process…selecting the right person for the job. Everything you've learned thus far will soon be put to use.

Buckle up and hang on tight. It's about to get bumpy!

Six Hoops and a Hire

There is nothing more costly in the staffing process than hiring the wrong person. Hiring the wrong person will reduce your productivity and your happiness. Hiring the wrong person will cause you to waste valuable time and energy training somebody who will eventually either quit or be fired. Hiring the wrong person is like signing up for a subscription to endless headaches, heartbreaks, and occasionally even lawsuits. You have already spent the time to learn the right role for your practice needs...now, under no circumstances, will I allow you to hire the wrong person to fill that role.

Our defense against a mis-hire is simple: *due diligence*. We will use every screening method within reason to narrow our field of applicants down, until we are left with just one terrific candidate. I call my recruiting due diligence process *Six Hoops and a Hire™* because we'll make our potential employees jump through not one, not two, but *six hoops* before offering them a job. And while that may seem like a bunch of work right now, a year from now when you've got a terrific employee doing amazing work, you'll know it was time well spent.

Hoop #1: Triage

We start in the simplest of ways. We will *triage*, or sort, your stack of resumes. Between Craigslist and other internet postings, staff referrals, client referrals and, perhaps, one to two people you spotted on your own, you may have anywhere from ten to forty resumes to choose from. This will vary based on position, salary offered, geographic location, and even the time of year, but somewhere in this range is where most readers will find themselves. And with these resumes, we will now create three basic piles: Yes, No, and Maybe.

The "No" pile is easiest, because there are several things that will immediately disqualify someone. Immediately place into this pile anyone who is geographically undesirable. While this may seem obvious, the Internet makes it easy for people in Des Moines to apply for jobs in San Diego. (If you're willing to consider relocating a candidate, then obviously an out-of-area address would not disqualify them.) The next resume group we want to eliminate are obvious job-hoppers. People don't stay at positions necessarily as long as they did a generation ago. But anyone who has had three or more jobs in as many years is too great a flight risk. Next—and this is especially necessary for Administrative Assistants—get rid of any resume with a typo, no matter how small. If they can't spell check a document as important as their own resume, they aren't careful enough to represent *you* to your clients. Another immediate red flag would be applicants who have never worked in an office environment. Some people really love "office work" and some do not. Generally, I look for people who already know they enjoy the inside-an-office environment.

The "Yes" pile is comprised of applicants who have worked within the financial services industry and performed similar duties to those you are hiring for, as well as people who have performed similar work in other industries. Hopefully, you've got one or two "jackpot!" resumes in this pile—say, someone who has several years of experience, securities registration and an insurance license. But don't limit the yes pile to these awesome candidates. Candidates from outside the industry but who have performed analogous work should be considered. I will almost always, for instance, consider a former loan processor to work in a business-processing role.

And the "Maybe" pile is essentially everybody else. Candidates who aren't disqualified by any of our "No" criteria, but might be a little soft in the experience department. Many of these applicants are not going to cut it, but for all you know someone in this pile might be average on paper but extremely strong in person.

So if you started with, say, twenty resumes, you typically would be really excited about one or two, have another couple 'yes' resumes, maybe a half dozen 'maybes,' and the rest 'no's. If you're a little worried that your three 'yes' candidates don't make for quite a large enough applicant pool (and this will probably be the case), you'll next want to return to the Maybe pile. Perhaps a few of these resumes are starting to look a little more viable. Pick the ones you feel best about, and when you've got about five or six resumes, you're ready to move on.

Hoop #2: Screening by Phone

It has always seemed logical to me that since you need to call an applicant anyway to invite them in for an interview, you might as well take an extra five minutes and screen for any red flags we didn't pick up from their resume. This is valuable because you're about to invest time and money testing and interviewing them. If you could avoid these costs by spending five minutes with them on the phone, it certainly makes sense to do so.

So we do a telephone screening. This is a "pre-interview interview" where we ask just three to six basic questions. Our goal is to screen out anybody who clearly lacks the poise, presence, or promise to handle a basic five-minute phone call.

Here's how to position the telephone screening so that you can gracefully *not* set an appointment with people who appear unqualified or pivot to the interview with people who sound strong. We open the call like this:

> *"Hi Jim, this is Lauren with ABC Financial Group. We received your resume, and are considering inviting a group of candidates in for interviews. I was wondering if you had a few minutes to answer just a few questions?" They'll say yes, and you'll ask them the questions you've got written out (yes, written out). If they turn out to be a disaster and you have no intention of spending time interviewing them, just close the call by saying "Jim, as I mentioned, we'll be getting back to a group of applicants soon. I want to thank you very much for your time." Conversely, you may close the call with a strong applicant simply by saying "Thanks Jim. I know you're going to be in our group of interview candidates, so why don't we go ahead and get an interview time scheduled?"*

The time you spend on a simple phone interview will help eliminate candidates who are unsuitable for the job while giving you a valuable head start with the applicants with whom you will be meeting in person.

Hoop #3: Screening Test

There is a multitude of screening tests available for employers to use. And if you had infinite time and money, and applicants had infinite patience, you would probably use them all. You would test for skill, intelligence, personality and instinct, giving yourself the broadest possible insight into the candidates you will be interviewing. But you don't have infinite time and money, and your applicants have lives that we must be respectful of, so we will limit ourselves to the most cost and time efficient forms of testing.

When I look at the selection process, it is completely logical to me to administer testing after you hear someone speak in a phone interview but before you invest time meeting him or her face to face. This is because most tests cost around $50, and most advisors doing testing make more than that an hour. But testing at this phase requires an advisor, or his representative, setting up the test beforehand, usually prepaying with a credit card, and for many advisors this level of effort is simply more than they are willing to expend. So most advisors who do use testing use it as a validation tool: after they've selected a final candidate, they test just to confirm their decision. And if you're wondering…yes, I think this is stupid. The tendency is to put too much emphasis on the test results if it confirms your positive instincts, or to disregard the test if it the applicant scores poorly but you've already fallen in love. If you're going to use testing, and I advise that all my readers do, then use it when it will count for something—before the interview. Better to invest $300 testing six applicants, and ending up with the best one, then to end up with someone who may not be the best candidate, then throw $50 down the drain on a test you're going to ignore anyway.

There are thousands of testing instruments available to you and the choice can be daunting. Generally, they fall into one of four buckets

– personality, skill, intelligence and psychometric. The test that has become almost a standard in our industry is the Kolbe 'A' Index. It falls into the psychometric category and if I were going to administer just one test, the Kolbe 'A' would be it.

The Kolbe measures innate striving instincts across four dimensions: *Fact-Finding* (how you gather and share information); *Follow-Thru* (how you sort and store information); *QuickStart* (how you deal with risks and uncertainty); and *Implementor* (how you handle space and tangibles). The "right" Kolbe for any particular job is a function of both the responsibilities for that position and the style of the manger. Generally speaking, for client service positions I look for strong Fact Finding and FollowThru ability. For administrators, I definitely want to see a high number in FollowThru, and for positions involving marketing I look for moderate to high numbers in QuickStart and strong FollowThru. For paraplanning and other technical positions, I look for people strong in Fact Finder. When it comes to practice managers, I've seen great managers with a range of Kolbe's but you'd probably hit the jackpot if you found one with mid-range scores across all four dimensions because that person could most easily "flex" to the styles of others and bring teams of people together.

You might want to consider the Kolbe's *Right Fit Program*. It's an inexpensive and indispensable selection tool that will help give you confidence in your hiring decisions. It consists of three components. First, a Kolbe 'A' assessment on you (remember the person you hire has to fit both the job and you), a Kolbe 'C' assessment through which you define the ideal candidate, and then Kolbe 'A' assessments on each candidate. The candidate is scored and you receive a report indicating whether she or he falls within an acceptable range.

There are hundreds of pre-employment assessment tools. I have a bias toward Kolbe. Whatever assessment you choose, please use it as an *aid* in your hiring decision but do not make your hiring decision based solely upon the results of a standardized test. The candidate's track record, how you felt about them in the interview, a "job audition" and reference checks should all be critical components of your hiring decision.

Also, be sure to use testing, and all screening tools, on a non-discriminatory basis. That means if you test one person between the telephone screening and face-to-face interview, then you must test all candidates whom you're considering interviewing at that same point in the process.

Hoop #4: The Interview

Between the phone interviews and the screening tests, you've probably eliminated two to three candidates. That leaves us with about four people to invite in for an interview.

I always feel that the first line of defense when it comes to judging applicants is the person working at your front desk. An Administrative Assistant or Receptionist can be a great second opinion, because they know who will fit well in the organization and they often get a glimpse of the candidate behavior before the candidate has put on their "interview face." When I worked at Lincoln Financial Advisors, our receptionist, Rina Cox, had been around for years and was an extremely shrewd judge of character. After every interview, we'd go out and ask Rina what she thought of the candidate. Sometimes she'd say, "Oh, I liked him a lot! He shook my hand and chatted with me warmly." Or she might say, "You know, she was a little abrupt. And as soon as she sat down, she took out her cell phone and started making calls. She didn't say goodbye on her way out." Character has been defined as "doing the right thing even when no one is looking." Rina rarely missed the mark. So if you have a Rina in your office, don't pass up that great screening tool—the gut feeling—of someone you trust.

Before you do any interviewing, get yourself a nice notebook, preferably one with a lined column on the right side and a blank space on the left. I recommend using the right side to record applicants' answers to questions, and in the blank margin you can jot down your thoughts or reactions. Whatever method feels most comfortable to you is fine...so long as you take a lot of notes. Don't be that person who thinks they can wing it, then struggles to remember the details of candidate responses.

When the actual interview begins, come out from behind your desk and sit next to the candidate. You can use the two guest chairs in front of your desk, a sofa and a chair, your conference table or a conference room. All of these options are fine but interviewing with a desk between you is never fine. It creates a psychological distance between you and the candidate that says, "I'm the boss." Which, of course, you are – but by the time you're done with this book you're going to know how to lead a team, not boss a team, and that's what we want to convey beginning on the day of the interview.

Which brings us to the meat and potatoes of the selection process: asking an applicant questions that will reveal their experience, strengths, style, poise and warts. From the Resource section of my website you can download my Interview Question Template. Now having an interview template is great — but please don't just pull out the questions and start interviewing. Knowing *how* to ask the questions is as important as the questions themselves.

I always start with a very basic question: "Tell me about yourself." This is such a broad and open-ended question that it actually takes quite a bit of poise on the part of the candidate to mentally assemble and prioritize the data points they think are most valuable. A side benefit to this question is you *sometimes* pick up information you couldn't otherwise glean – personal information about family and background – which may say a lot about the person, but is outside the bounds of what you can ask about. From my website you can download a lsit of *No-No Questions* — questions and topics you are *not* permitted to address in an interview.

Another good question to ask early: "So, what brings you to the job marketplace?" It's a disarmingly simple question and forces an applicant to be reasonably honest. Are they unemployed? Do they feel underpaid? Under-challenged? Under-recognized? If they like their job, why then do they want to move on?

Just like when you're taking data from clients, during an interview you want to spend 80% of time in listen mode. If you're doing the talking, you're not learning anything. And the more effective you become at delving the more you're going to learn. There is an interview technique called "layering" and I encourage you to master it. Let's say you asked a candidate to tell you about the most challenging project they ever worked on. They answer you. Layering questions might include:

> *"It sounds like that project had a lot of moving parts. How did you organize it all?"*

> *"Were you able to accomplish that project in the context of your regular job or did you have to put in extra time?"*

> *"What about that project was particularly rewarding to you?"*

> *"What would you do differently next time?"*

> *"What did your manager do or not do that impacted the outcome of the project?"*

Do you see that? Five revealing 'twig' questions off the 'branch' question: "Tell me about your most challenging project." There have been many times that I've interviewed someone so polished that they glided through most questions with ease. But my layering questions – asked with a tone of real curiosity and no judgment – often hit a nerve. And I got answers that sounded like these: "Well, what the customer wanted was impossible and I told them so." Or "it wasn't my responsibility anyway. It was Mark's responsibility because he handled booking." Or "they gave me the project, they expected me to handle everything and I didn't get any help." *Pay dirt* – red flag, red flag, red flag.

A favorite question of mine, and one that I never skip is, "Tell me about the best boss you ever had." Candidates will answer in a number of ways but, invariably, the essence of the responses fall into one of two groups. Either they'll say "I loved that he would give me work, but be supportive when I had questions or wanted to discuss things further," or "I loved that he just gave me work, and got out of my way." There's no right or wrong answer here…just valuable insight into whether the candidate's needs match your management style. If you tend to be very detail-oriented and hands-on, look for a person who likes a boss who is accessible for questions and support. If you prefer to delegate completely and have your staff come back with a finished product, you will do better with the "let me run with it" candidate.

Hoop #5: Job Audition

Years ago, I was conducting interviews for the receptionist position at our San Ramon, California office. I was interviewing a young woman named Indaoli when the temporary, who was handling our then vacant front desk, knocked on the door. She said, "Lauren, there's a gentleman on the phone…I don't know what he's saying because he's speaking Spanish, but I can tell he's very upset." I was asking myself aloud "Who's here today that speaks Spanish…?" when Indaoli said quietly, "I speak Spanish." I asked Indaoli if she'd be comfortable, with me at her side, talking to the caller. She said she was so we put her on the phone, she quickly introduced herself, found out what the client needed, and with a little bit of back and forth coaching and translation, the upset client was soothed. Naturally I hired Indaoli, who became a wonderful asset to the organization.

That experience made me realize that there could be no better predictor of how someone will perform on a job then to administer a "job audition." Since that day, I have been a firm believer in the use of *job auditions*. As you saw in the example above, a job audition is when you ask an applicant to perform a standard duty that they would do every day if hired for the job. Now, that doesn't mean I have an angry Spaniard call the office in the middle of every interview – although that would be a heckuva test. What's my test for an Administrative Assistant? Typically, I'll give them a client fact-finder or computer screen and ask them to transfer information, as best they can, to a blank brokerage application. I'll leave them "sign here" stickers and ask them to place a sticker everywhere the client should sign. Finally,

I'll ask them to type a cover letter to be mailed with the application to the client.

What will I find out from the job audition? First, I'll find out how much common sense and intelligence the candidate has as they work with two unfamiliar items – the fact finder and the brokerage app. Next I'll learn whether the candidate can find Microsoft Word on the computer. I'll also find out if they know how to format a business letter – block style with the correct number of lines between date, address, salutation, body and signature. I'll find out whether they use Spell Check. Most importantly, I'll find out if they can compose a lucid and professional-looking letter. Finally, I'm going to know whether they can they do all of this in a reasonable amount of time (under 40 minutes, start to finish, is good), under fire. (Not that there are ever any fires in our business!)

Job auditions don't have to be particularly creative or abstract. For a ParaPlanner applicant, you may just sit them down at a computer, show them your planning software, and ask them to enter data from a data form into the program. If they are unfamiliar with the program, get them started, and see how well they figure it out. They might not be perfect, but you'll know if they're a quick learner. Seeing somebody do something is a lot better than listening to them tell you that they can!

But don't confine yourself to these examples. You know what your staff does on a daily basis…design a simple job audition for it. Are you hiring a Concierge who will have to set appointments? Well, have the applicant call a pretend client (another staff person can be this person) to set an appointment. Give them your calendar and give them three specific date/time ranges within which to make the appointment. Instruct the staff person to be a little resistant. What will you see? You'll see willingness to pick up a phone, tone of voice, resilience and resourcefulness. Not bad for a three minute test!

Hoop #6: Reference Check

We're on the due diligence home stretch! You (or better yet, your Practice Manager) has sorted resumes, administered tests and interviewed your way down to two candidates. Now it's time to check references. Many people will say that because everyone is so liability-conscious these days, former employers won't give you any good information on applicants and, thus, reference checks are useless. There is some truth to this belief. Many companies, especially big ones, instruct their people to verify only name, position title and dates of employment. But this I know: If an employer *loved* an employee, they will give a reference. So here's a tried and true reference checking strategy.

Call the reference at a time when they're unlikely to be in the office (maybe 6am or 9pm), and leave this message:

> *"This is Doug from South Coast Financial Group. We're interviewing Margie Bryant for a key administrative role on our team. Would you please call me back <u>only</u> if Margie was an exceptional employee."*

If they loved Margie, they'll call back, and you'll know two things: Margie was an exceptional employee, and she probably left under good terms.

Another "unofficial" way to learn about someone is to use the Internet. I "Google" people's names all the time…it only takes a second and you never know what will pop up. An editorial they wrote in college, their official time running the LA Marathon, a picture of the heavy metal band they play in on weekends…if it helps you make a decision, why not use it? And many younger applicants are on *MySpace* or *Facebook*, social networking sites that allow members to post a virtual A to Z description of themselves, their friends, and their lifestyles. For instance, you would never ask an applicant if they like to get drunk and snowboard naked, but you might see a photo of them doing exactly that on *MySpace*. What people post on the Internet reflects their pursuits, priorities and judgment.

If the candidate is or was securities registered, definitely check the CRD record on the FINRA website: http://www.finra.org/Investors/ToolsCalculators/BrokerCheck/index.htm

The reason I check references at the very end is that, if you're in a coin toss situation between two great candidates, you can use the reference check to push you one way or another. But the reference check is just one of the tools at your disposal in this process, and you shouldn't base your decision on any one of the hoops alone. When it gets down to two applicants, don't just use your *head*…you may pick someone with more experience, or more licenses, but less charm. And don't just use your *heart*…a nice personality and pretty smile alone does not a terrific employee make. No, I tell people to make this decision with their *gut*. Your gut is your best friend. If anything didn't feel quite right about an applicant, if they didn't respond enthusiastically when they came back for a second interview, if they weren't animated or didn't smile, if they never asked you questions about the job or the office, or if they put you off in any way…don't make them an offer. After all, this person has ostensibly been trying their hardest to seem as likable as possible during the hiring process. Trust me, this is them at their best. If you don't like them now, they're not going to get any better. And if your gut tells you not to hire either candidate, then don't. Tough it out for another few weeks until you find the right person. Being on your own for one more moment without support may be costly and draining. But hiring the wrong person is a whole other level of misery. So your gut is the boss. Listen to the boss.

Well, good work! You've just completed a crash course on candidate selection, and mastered the six hoops. And now, as promised, we get to the easy part…the hire!

The Offer Letter

You've gone through resumes, interviews, reference, and gut checks and finally selected the candidate you want to add to your team. The hard work is out of the way. But bear with me. There's just one last formality to take care of.

An *Offer Letter* is a tool that far too few advisors use, but one that I recommend because it accomplishes several things. First, it's a nice, professional way to start a relationship. It shows your new employee that they're joining the ranks of a team that has their stuff together. It also creates structure right off the bat - structure that will endure for the rest of their employment. And finally, an offer letter provides a modicum of protection for you in what we hope is the unlikely event that you hired a person who develops performance issues. (Notice I said a "modicum" of protection – the offer letter helps you document *some* fundamental employment details). Essentially, an offer letter is a way to set the tone for a great working relationship…before a new employee even begins working. You'll find a template for this letter on my website.

The Offer Letter document represents the end of your search, the fulfillment of time invested in finding the right person and placing them in the right role. Enjoy the moment! In the third section of this book, we'll explore the final component of the equation…*keeping* the exceptional people you've hired. You do not have to suffer through the abysmal employee turnover that plagues so many careers in our industry. I'm going to show you how to never get fired as a boss and to retain the amazing talent you've worked so hard to find.

So, meet me at the next chapter, where for the first time we're not going to be working on staffing…we're going to be working on *you*.

The Ten Currencies

About Currencies

In the first section of this book, you developed an understanding of *The Dream Team* staffing concept and the talents required for each *Dream Team* role. In the second section of the book, you learned a due diligence process for recruiting great talent for your team. Now we're on the home stretch and the final section of this book is dedicated to *retaining* the exceptional staff that you have or will recruit. And how do you retain exceptional staff?

The simple answer is "don't get fired as the boss."

Yes, bosses get fired every day. They get fired by employees whose expectations are not being met. Many of my clients are initially surprised when I ask them about the "employee experience" at their firms. They usually say something like, "Lauren, everyone here is focused on the client experience, not the employee experience." And, if that's the case, it's the first thing I set out to change. Because where employees stick, clients stick. And the best way to get employees to stick is to use every "currency" at your disposal.

And I have ten perfectly wonderful currencies for you to use. Not every currency will be effective with every employee – but the right combination of currencies will always be effective.

Don't feel badly if, until just now, you had no idea there were nine things other than money your employees wanted from you. When you're done with this book, you can go ahead and pay them retroactively! But since cash is the carrot on which most advisors focus, we'll start there.

Currency #1

Cold Hard Cash

When people look for jobs, they pay a lot of attention to salary. As well they should…money makes the world go 'round. It pays for our food, shelter, our cars, our plasma TVs, our vacations, our children's college education. Monetary compensation is fundamental to the employment process, and I certainly don't mean to diminish its importance. But money is also *obvious* - people expect to get paid. Unless you're a volunteer, money is a given when going to work for eight hours, and the money you're shelling out is the same color as your competition's in the employment market. So how do you distinguish your money from his when enticing and retaining employees?

You might not like to hear it, but the answer is simple: Pay your employees 20-30% more than the guy down the street, and they won't leave you because of money. For those of you who have always attempted to "get the most for the least" this advice may seem insane. But smooth your ruffled feathers, please, and consider the quantifiable benefits. First, if you advertise a very competitive salary range in your job postings, you'll attract a larger pool of candidates. More candidates means more choices and a greater likelihood of finding your nearly perfect person. Second, that person will feel appropriately valued from day one. They will likely then focus on the objectives of their employment rather than the conditions of their employment. They will be more satisfied, overall, with their employment and more likely to become long-term employees. This will save you hundreds of thousands of dollars over your career since you will not have to spend your precious time constantly recruiting, training and performing employee tasks.

If you're not sure what the folks down the street are paying, check out the free salary research tools at salary.com. All you do is type in a job title and zip code and you'll get a listing of job titles and descriptions and one of them will likely be close to the position you're recruiting.

Bonuses

In addition to salary, the other compensation tool we have at our disposal is bonuses. Right off the bat, I'll tell you there is a kind of bonus I like and a kind I don't like. The kind I don't like is a subjective bonus, paid at the end of the year, for no particular reason. The check may be large one year and smaller the next and in either case the staff may be confused as to why it changed. And after you've paid the bonus one time—just one time—even the best employees will tend to regard it as an entitlement. If you pay someone a $2,000 bonus one year and try to skip it the next, believe me, you are going to have a very unhappy employee. Now, I'm not saying employers shouldn't give a holiday gift…a few hundred dollars, a beautiful present, whatever you feel is appropriate. But a true bonus should be given to staff members who helped you achieve results in a measurable way, and should always be conditional on such. Salary is an *entitlement*. Bonuses are an *incentive*.

Now, I've developed several hundred bonuses over the years. Some of them were pretty good, and others were doomed to failure. There's no one "perfect bonus formula" that I can give you that will be effective in every practice or with every individual. But what I can give you are some tips I've gleaned from my experiences with incentive compensation over the years. No matter how you structure your bonus, make sure it meets the following four requirements:

1. **Easy to understand.** Many times I'll ask an advisor, "Tell me about your incentive program." Then they start fumbling. "Well, it based on growth…no, revenue and growth. Errr…actually it has more to do with our company honors program…" STOP. You've said enough. If you don't know exactly what your bonus is based on, your staff probably doesn't either. For an incentive to work, your staff has to know exactly what they need to do to get rewarded. "If I do more X, I'll make more money." If you can't tell me what X is, the bonus won't work.

2. **Easy to calculate.** You shouldn't need to call in Ernst & Young each month to figure out how much to pay people.

Years ago, when I was Operations Manager at Lincoln Financial, I decided I wanted to make more money. So I approached my bosses, Nick Horn and Ted Santon, and asked if we could restructure my compensation. Great bosses that they were, Nick and Ted came up with an incentive plan. My salary each year equaled 2% of the gross revenue of the previous year. In addition, I received two objective bonuses. The first bonus was equal to 2% of the year-over-year revenue growth from the previous year. The second bonus was equal to 2% of the net profits. Two, two, and two. So simple even a non-numbers girl like me could easily grasp it. Most importantly, being paid this way made me feel and act like an owner.

3. **Rewards team effort.** When the business is doing well, the entire staff should share in the bounty. There is nothing more annoying to employees than seeing their boss make more and more money while their salaries remain the same. If the firm is making more money, then everyone on the team should have the opportunity to be rewarded. This includes people who impact the top line through marketing and sales and the people who impact the bottom line by freeing you up to develop new business. When your assistant pushes business through underwriting like a pit bull, she's impacting your bottom line. When your ParaPlanner saves you hours of prep time on an investment review, she's impacting your bottom line. When your Concierge gets you that appointment with a referral, she's impacting your bottom line. If you did well this year, it's in no small part due to the efforts of your team. This is a team game. Giving everyone on the team a bonus based on growth in revenue, clients or profit, is a way of saying "I couldn't have done this without you. Thanks." In fact, that's exactly what you should say when you hand them the check.

4. **Rewards individual effort.** In addition to rewarding everyone based on the results of the practice, the bonus should reward individual performance. We want to take care of everybody when times are good, but we're still capitalists here. People who perform best should be compensated best. So there should be a component of the bonus for which employees

individually strive. For the Concierge position, we might establish a bonus for "kept appointments" with prospects. For the Advisor Assistant position, we might establish a bonus for getting cases through underwriting or investment transfers completed in X amount of time. Another idea to reward individual performance is by encouraging employees to come up with significant quarterly projects (approved by you) and paying them $1,000 or so for successful completion of each. Projects that lend themselves to this structure include conversion to a paperless office, designing a process, documentation of procedures or coordinating a marketing campaign. Individual bonuses are all about figuring out how each employee can enrich the client experience, save you time or grow revenue.

One of the simplest incentives I've encountered that meets all four requirements, I learned from an extremely successful advisor. This advisor had a staff of three – but you can adapt this bonus for any size staff. In any month where he earned between $50,000 and $60,000, his staff evenly divided a pool of $1,000. But in any month where the advisor earned over $60,000, he took 10% of the excess above $60,000 and paid it out *subjectively* to whomever had made the biggest contributions that month. It might go to someone who pushed a case through underwriting, or coordinated a great client appreciation event, but it always went to someone who went above and beyond. This bonus rewards both team results and personal achievement, is simple to understand and simple to administer. You can count on end-of-month enthusiasm when you have an incentive like this in place.

Here are a few more bonus coaching tips:

Frequent is better. The more frequently an incentive is paid, the more motivating it is. Bonuses, particularly for lower-salary positions, should be paid no less often than once a quarter. This has several benefits. People like money sooner rather than later. Even staff members making in excess of $100K a year may have cash flow issues, and getting a check monthly or quarterly can really be a great motivator. Even more important is that paying bonuses at more frequent intervals forces you to focus on measuring your results – good, bad or ugly. And the sooner you and your team focus on results, the more likely you are to make adjustments that can impact those results.

The bonus must be significant. An incentive that is too small is like no incentive at all. In fact, it can be a demotivator. The next time an employee is making a decision about whether to put in some "above and beyond" effort they may just say, "Eh, forget it. So I don't make my five hundred bucks at the end of the year. I'd rather just leave early." Sometimes the line gets even blurrier, and they're not only shirking work that could get them a bonus, they're doing shoddy work on tasks you absolutely *expect* of them. However, the opposite is true as well. The energy and excitement generated by substantial bonuses can be contagious. So for any bonus to be motivating, I suggest that its potential be at least 10% of the salary for administrative roles, and in the 20-30% for the professional roles on your team.

Every bonus must be achievable. Your bonuses should be based on reasonable growth targets and be completely achievable. Don't bother with "stretch" goals – they always complicate and rarely work. And, if you're offering a project bonus, then you need to make sure that that bonus is also reasonably achievable.

Not every employee responds to cash. I bet you know lots of people that don't change their behavior no matter how fabulous the cash carrot is. In fact, there's nothing more useless than a cash bonus for an employee not motivated by money. But sometimes these people are turned on by rewards in lieu of cash. Some of my clients have rewarded employees with two-week European vacations, lovely jewelry or even a significant contribution to a college fund for a child or grandchild. For employees who crave work/life balance and travel, additional time off can replace a cash bonus.

For an employer, a big bonus is preferable to a big salary. The reason for this is obvious. You want to keep your fixed costs as low as possible. I know, I know…I told you to pay 20% to 30% more than the guys down the street and now I'm telling you to keep your fixed costs down. The reason your opening salaries have to be higher than the competition is it's very hard to convince a new employee – a virtual stranger to the practice – that an incentive can make good financial sense. They *hope* they've hitched their wagon to the right star but there's no proof that they have. But after a year of working together – a year in which they've seen your results – your career minded employees will be attracted to a comp plan with tremendous upside potential. Just like I was when my bosses offered me the 2/2/2 plan.

All incentives should be in writing. If you absolutely must, you can ignore every rule I've just provided and go off and create your own crazy incentive formulas. Cram that baby with as many square roots and fractals as you wish. But please, please, please, put the whole thing in writing, and include two things: First, state that in order to receive the bonus the employee must be in good standing. This way you will never be obligated to pay an incentive to an employee who is in a verbal or written warning period. Second, state that the incentive period is from January 1st to December 31st. You can, and often will, renew the terms of an incentive year after year. But if the incentive you created was for any reason not getting you the results you desired, you don't want to be married to it. Set a term for the program and junk it if it isn't working.

We review compensation agreements with each employee every year at their formal evaluation meetings. Since these meetings usually take place in January, it forces us to focus on compensation and practice objectives when we do our business plans in November and December.

If you make the monetary rewards rewarding enough, your people probably won't leave you for more money. But that doesn't mean that's all you have to do. There are nine other currencies that will glue great employees to your practice.

And they're almost entirely free.

Career Path

I can still remember quite clearly my first day working in the financial planning industry. It was 1984, and I had just been hired as a very green Operations Manager for the San Francisco branch of (what was then) The New England Mutual Life Insurance Company. On that first day, the General Agent did something that really got my attention. He sat me down and showed me a neatly typed page, divided into three columns. The first column was my current role as Operations Manager, listing the duties, competencies, salary, bonuses and key areas of focus. The second column indicated a progressively more challenging role as Director of Operations. And the third column— which really got my attention—was titled "Co-General Agent." I didn't know a whole life policy from a hole in the wall, but I could tell that title represented a big opportunity that could be mine.

By showing me what lay ahead, that General Agent did something special. He wasn't just offering me a job. He was offering me a *career*. And there are many focused, bright individuals who not only appreciate the distinction, they expect it. Perhaps in times past, that was simply not something a financial advisor could offer. When I walked into that New England office those many years ago, most advisors had one assistant, who, if the advisor were lucky, would stick around. But the idea that an assistant had any real career mobility would have been a tough concept to sell. But this isn't 1984, and thanks to *The Dream Team* staffing model, there's no employee to whom you'll offer a job that you cannot also offer a career.

But before you can tell your employees about the career paths available to them, you first need to understand them yourself. And, if you've were paying attention when we talked about roles and genes, it should be pretty intuitive.

The Basics

In the first section of the book where we discussed the traits we look for in an Assistant, I told you there were two genes that were absolutely mandatory: the organizational gene and the nurturing gene. And for a ParaPlanner, those genes are less important; the fundamental piece of DNA required to do *that* job is the analytical gene. And if you were paying attention during the second section of the book, hiring the right people for these distinct roles shouldn't be too hard.

But what happens if you hire an assistant who, in between keeping your client data perfectly organized and looking after you, is fascinated by the power of an *Intentionally Defective Insurance Trust* or who pours over your CFP® study materials? Maybe they ask you for advice on managing their own investment account and you notice their return is better than yours! These are all hallmarks of someone who, though they may have a *dominant* gene in nurturing or organization, have a *recessive* analytical gene. You may have noticed it the first time you interviewed them, or it may have lay dormant for years. But this person has analytical abilities lying just below the surface, and now you've got to decide what to do with them.

The Dream Team is structured so that an Administrative Assistant with strong technical ability can and should be groomed for a promotion to ParaPlanner. If they demonstrate an interest in and inclination toward technical work, start by giving them more responsibility in plan manufacture, investment review prep and research. The Insurance and Investment Support Specialist roles we discussed earlier in the book are good examples of ways to utilize assistants with analytical talents. If they do well, you may move on to getting them insurance licensed or securities registered. Assuming they meet your expectations, a promotion to ParaPlanner may be in order, provided the position is available (we'll talk more about this shortly).

The same is true of an Assistant who seems to have a recessive social gene. Do your clients rave about your Assistant's customer service skills? Maybe you got a call from your assistant's dentist…apparently, he or she pitched your services to them and now they want to come in to talk with you. An assistant like this with a flare for marketing may be the perfect candidate for the Concierge position.

I love these recessive genes because they allow us to do something that is almost always advantageous – promoting from within. As good as our screening methods are, why go out and hire someone unproven when there's an opportunity right in your own back yard? In addition to eliminating the need for the screening process, you hire someone already intimately familiar with your process, your team, and most importantly, with you.

So, for any Administrative Assistant with strong technical or marketing ability, a possible career path looks like this:

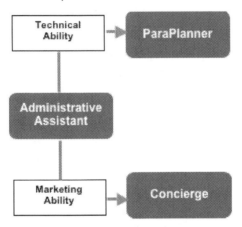

Now, let's think about another recessive gene, one you might not notice until your staff expands. Perhaps you've given your ParaPlanner of several years more responsibility. They've moved from manufacturing plans and prepping investment reviews to case design and investment analysis. You've got so much work you've brought in a second ParaPlanner to perform front-end data entry on plans, prepare quarterly investment reports, and do research. You've begun grooming future ParaPlanners through an intern program. And all of a sudden, that technical wiz you hired to crunch numbers is doing something you had never envisioned...managing this staff of ParaPlanners, and managing them well. This ParaPlanner, it seems, had a recessive management gene. The same may be found of a Concierge who is a natural managing the group of marketing interns you brought in to help her. In both cases, you may have excellent Practice Manager material on your hands.

And don't exclude your Administrative Assistant from the management mix. I have on many, many occasions promoted assistants straight to Practice Managers, provided they have demonstrated that "take charge" management ability. Often, the assistant makes an especially logical choice for the Practice Manager role because they are the person in the practice most trusted by the advisor, and with whom the advisor is most comfortable. So when we update our career path chart to reflect the Practice Manager, it now looks like this:

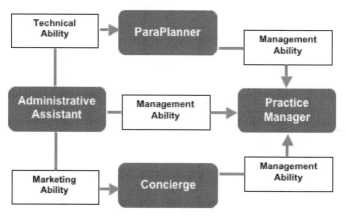

But we're not done yet.

Let's say you've got a ParaPlanner who has been with you for several years. They've earned their CFP® or CIMA® designation, and now have a small staff working under them. And they come to you and say something like this: "Bill, I've done some analysis, and I've identified thirty clients we have on the XYZ Asset Management Program platform. I'd like to suggest that we bring these clients in, and you and I talk to them about the opportunity of investing in the ABC program as well. I believe this would be a tremendous opportunity for this group of clients and I project that we'd pick up between $25 and $50 million in new assets."

A ParaPlanner who can both see and seize an opportunity may be a candidate for promotion to a position we haven't discussed in quite a while: the *Junior*, or *Associate* Advisor. You may have, right from within your ranks, the perfect Associate Advisor to help you take your business to its next level.

One day, your Concierge comes to you with an idea. He or she has done some research, and discovered the following: "Bill, we have sixty clients with sizeable accounts, and you're not getting in touch with them. Specifically, I've identified forty-five clients that you haven't seen in five years, but have potential to be strong B, and possibly, A clients. I'd like to write a letter to these clients, introducing myself, then follow up with another letter and a phone call. Let's see if we can't get these people in here and talk to them about our expanded team and services." This Concierge could be clueless when it comes to the technical stuff, but they're fearless when it comes to asking for business. Here, again, is a candidate within your practice for Associate Advisor.

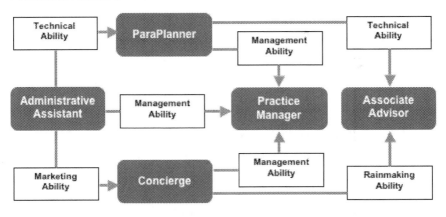

Can your Practice Manager become your Junior? The short answer is yes, although true management ability is rare, and most practices desperately need a Practice Manager as much or more than an Associate Advisor. Rather than make a good Practice Manager a full-fledged Associate Advisor, a shrewder move might be a promotion to an "inside partner." So, although I have seen a few Practice Managers move into production, I do not actively promote this as a career path.

So when we put this all together, your have a pretty exciting future to present to every member of your *Dream Team*. Have a look:

Career Path: Application

Now that we have discussed the fundamentals of career mobility within *The Dream Team*, we can discuss the practical application of such a system. And as always, something that looks pretty on paper may not always work in practice. In particular, there are two facts that may have occurred to you while reading, which we will discuss now.

Fact #1: Not everybody wants or needs a career path.

Just as there are employees who aren't particularly motivated by money, there are employees who just aren't looking for a career path. There are many wonderful assistants out there who are quite content to spend the duration of their careers in the same role being rewarded with competitive compensation. You may offer them more money if they will get their Series 6, CFP®, or insurance license, but you'll find they just drag their heels. They're not interested, and so this won't be an effective currency to use. You'll do better to look elsewhere for recruiting other positions.

Fact #2: An employee may want a career path but you may not have one to offer. Well let's rephrase that. You have the career path identified, but you may not have the immediate need or resources to move an employee up that career path. Presenting a career path to an employee does not require you to prematurely promote them. To move to the next level on their career path they must both meet the requirements for that role and the business must have a need for that role.

If all this talk about career paths seems a little bizarre to you because you picked up this book hoping to hire your first employee, don't tune out. A career path is as important before the career begins as it is after. By showing a brand new Administrative Assistant a career path, you do something special. A lot of people can talk about room for growth, but if you only have one employee, it's a tough pitch to sell. Committing it to paper makes it real. It demonstrates that you invest time in strategic planning and that you're committed to growing the members of your team.

One final point...

In the war for talent you may find yourself competing with larger firms. To the uninitiated, these firms – with multi-level hierarchies – may seem appealing. But *you* have a compelling story to tell. What are the value points you're selling? They might be that you have a track record of progressive growth; your *Dream Team* is light and nimble, and you're not hamstrung by levels of management. You can take ideas and run with them. A young person joining a vibrant practice today is likely to make more money, have more fun and enjoy greater control than just about anywhere else. And if I were interviewing a promising young candidate for your firm tomorrow, that's exactly what I'd tell them!

Currency #3

Training

Welcome to Stroock & Levin Financial, a company with a tradition of excellence in the Baltimore area for over 15 years. If you've made it this far, you, no doubt, have been through a rigorous selection process, and have proven yourself to be of exemplary character, experience and ability. Before you can fully function as a member of our team, however, we must insist that you complete our mandatory training program (manual enclosed on next page). We look forward to working with you!

STROOK & LEVIN FINANCIAL SERVICES

TRAINING MANUAL FOR NEW EMPLOYEES

1. Find your desk.
2. Sit at your desk.
3. Work

Our friends at the firm of *Stroock & Levin* are fictional but the challenge of training new employees is very real. With few exceptions, our industry is virtually bereft of adequate training programs for new employees. Because of this, our national *de facto* training program is "baptism by fire." Some people survive this training program, but sadly, many do not. We can do much better. We must do much better. Because training is not just a formality in the hiring process, it is a currency with which we pay our staff. And skimping on it is like paying minimum wage for the first three months...you're going to end up alienating, and perhaps losing, some good people along the way.

I'm not going to use this chapter to outline the finer points of Microsoft Excel or talk about downloading Morningstar snapshots. And I don't have the knowledge of your specific infrastructure to talk about the special way your staff needs to load paper into the copier so it doesn't jam. But what I can do is show you that, even if you believe that you currently have no training resources whatsoever, you actually *do* have training tools at your disposal. And when it comes to training, something is far better than nothing.

Orientation

After investing weeks – perhaps months – in recruiting the newest member of your *Dream Team*, you're desperate to finally be able to refocus on your business. So there's a predictable tendency to immediately start throwing work at your new employee. You did such a good job analyzing your *Dream Team* needs and selecting the ideal candidate, I'm hoping I can get you to invest just a little more time in assuring a healthy return on your investment. So, please…hold off with training on application prep, filing and data entry. There's something far more important for your new employee to immediately learn. Your employee needs to learn "what's important around here."

What's important in your practice? This has to do with the brand you're building. What's important to you may be your planning approach; your service team concept; your concierge service or your innovative marketing. Whatever makes your practice special, I want your new employees to understand it before they ever do a lick of work. When employees understand what's important to you, they're able to make good decisions on your behalf.

So use the first couple of days with a new employee to transfer a macro understanding of your business. I've found that the easiest way to do this is to introduce a new employee to your business the same way you would a client. They should see how you conduct business, from the bottom up and top down. Most advisors—and bosses in general—just insert a new employee in what seems like a logical section of the business, without filling them in on the big picture. They assume a ParaPlanner doesn't need to know anything about marketing, or a Concierge needn't have a clue about number crunching. But by showing them the grand scheme, you include them on the broad vision of the practice…the scope of what's important to you can't be found in any one corner of the office. It's everywhere.

I suggest starting the orientation where the business process starts: finding new clients. Tell a new employee how this is done. For most of you, that's through referrals. If you have a specific referral process, tell them about it here and make sure they understand how important those introductions are. If you market through seminars or centers of influence, talk about those systems here as well.

Once you get a client, the next thing you likely do is analyze their needs. You probably do that by creating financial and investment plans. So here is where I'd suggest showing a new employee what those plans look like. Briefly walk them through the software that created it. Again, this isn't just for ParaPlanners…I want Assistants and Concierges to see this aspect of the business too.

Next, we generally come to implementation. Explain to your newest staff member how you represent the client in the marketplace and help them purchase insurance and investments. You might talk about the primary investment platforms that you use, and insurance carriers with whom you most frequently place business.

Once we're past implementation, our focus shifts to service. And I want you to make a big fuss about client service, no matter what position you are training. Because exceptional client service should be on everybody's mind. In this section, discuss how you segment your clients into A, B, and C categories, and what services you provide each of these segments.

If there are any other big picture items you want your employees to be familiar with, be sure to fit them in as well. Two that I would always include would be compliance and metrics – how you keep score as you grow your business. And, for sure, I'd be talking about the behaviors that you value (also known as competencies). These might include initiative, accountability, attention to detail, organization, customer focus and teamwork.

One important note about these first couple days of "macro" orientation - this task should *not* be delegated. If you have a tenured person on your staff, you can and should turn over the nitty-gritty, functional training. But the biggest, most powerful messages should come from you. So keep your new employee close during the first few days. Take them with you to a client meeting, go to lunch, and generously share your perspective on your business. Your investment in time will pay off. I promise.

I was the Vice President of the San Ramon branch of Lincoln Financial Advisors for many years. This organization had over 200 advisors and 75 staff. I had people to whom I could delegate employee training. But whenever we hired a new receptionist, I wanted to be the one to sit with them for their first two days. Why? Because I believed this position was extraordinarily important and I wanted to make sure this belief was transferred to the new receptionist. I wanted those receptionists to smile a certain way, answer phones a certain way, receive clients a certain way. "Press this button when the phone rings and then press the extension" could wait. The receptionist was our *Director of First Impressions*. There were important messages to be delivered and I wanted to be the person to deliver them.

Create A Training Outline

With a couple days of big picture orientation behind us, we're ready to begin the work of training our new employee on the specific functions of the position. I've discovered that there are two ways to do this. One is to just meander through the duties in no particular order, with no specific starting point and no well-defined end. You'd never "train" a new client that way, so why train the person who will serve your clients this way? The alternative, which I suggest, is simply to use a *training outline*.

You're moaning now. I can hear it. You're saying, "After losing the better part of eight weeks to recruiting, and the last two days to that

'What's Important Around Here' orientation, now she wants me to sit down and create a training outline?" Yeah, I do. Actually, I prefer someone do this for you but, either way, you've already done the heavy lifting because your training outline is going to come right from the job description you created before beginning your search. For every responsibility on that job description, some training should be provided. So all you have to do to create a training outline is pluck categories and responsibilities from the job description and place them in order of training priority, then add columns for who will deliver the training and when. So the training outline will look like this:

Category	Responsibility	Trainer	Date
Investment Processing	Process new account paperwork	Mary	10/15
Investment Processing	Respond to "Not in Good Order" issues	Mary	10/16
Investment Processing	Prepare weekly investment account status report	Mary	10/16
Insurance Processing	Prepare VUL applications	Janice	10/20
Insurance Processing	Follow-up on outstanding underwriting requirements	Janice	10/21

The Training Template

So now you have your training outline for your new employee and various members of your team are now going to sit down with your newbie to transfer knowledge and develop skills. After years of watching people train and learn, I'm convinced that most people are not natural trainers. Some people give too much information, others not enough. Almost all either start or end the training in the wrong place.

To even out these inevitable inconsistencies in training, I've developed an extraordinarily simple training template that our clients use across the board. We teach everyone to train in this exact format:

Subject: "Here's what I'm going to train you on today"

Category: This subject falls under the category of X

Resources: "Here's what you need to perform this function" (forms, data, etc.)

Steps: "Here are the steps – 1,2,3."

Contacts: "Here's contact info for the people who can help you with this function (at the broker-dealer, insurance carrier or OSJ)

You'll find this training template on my website. If you consistently train in this way and require your trainees to immediately type up the instructions using the template, then, guess what? Not only will you have accomplished the training of a single employee, you will have developed a procedures manual for every future employee! You and your staff will be amazed at how beautifully this training system works.

30 For 90

New employees will have questions. That's a given. What isn't a given is how effectively you'll respond to those questions.

The simplest way to handle this issue is to set aside thirty minutes a day to answer questions during the first ninety days of a new staff member's employment. If you have a Practice Manager, then *30 for 90* will fall to them. If it's you and you're in the office you can do this in person; if you're out you can do it by phone. Some days your new employee may have thirty minutes of questions, but on most days they will not. The questions will become fewer with each passing day. Your investment of time will pay off. Work will be accomplished faster. You'll suffer fewer potentially embarrassing errors. Your new employee will gain in confidence because they'll never feel totally stranded and you'll eliminate those "Got a minute?" interruptions because you will have trained the new employee to batch their questions.

I had one client who said, "I may know the answers but that doesn't mean I want to be the reference librarian." And I understood exactly how he felt. If you're worried that *30 for 90* constitutes too much handholding, don't be. Being available to your new employee at a set time every day doesn't mean that you have to spoon-feed them the answers. This is the optimum time to begin building empowerment, judgment and self-reliance. If an employee asks a question and it's high time they should either know the answer or know where to go to get it, you'll say, "What do *you* think you have to do in this situation?" Nine times out of ten, they will know the right answer and all you have to do is say, "Bingo – that's it!" Even after the first 90 days are passed, never forget this tip because if all answers come from you, you will never have the empowered, take-charge team you need.

Delegate Training

As I've already stated, *you* should conduct the orientation, *you* should have final sign-off on the training outline and *you* should be available to answer questions, as needed. But everything else? Please…go ahead and delegate it.

We lean on others during the training process for a bunch of reasons. The biggest is to leverage your time. But even if time weren't an issue, you aren't necessarily the most proficient person in your office at every particular task. So let the experienced members of your team pick up the training slack.

Are you lacking experience within your own office to train a new employee? This is common, especially with smaller practices, as you may be hiring a position that did not exist previously in your organization. One way around this obstacle is to seek help from your peers. If you have a buddy who has a good assistant, Practice Manager or ParaPlanner, ask if you can buy a little of their time for a few hours to mentor your new employee. If they're on the fence, remind them that everybody gets better when they teach someone else and you'll return the favor.

Licensing and Industry Training

I absolutely believe financial planners should encourage their employees to seek industry training and licensing…but not right away. The reason I mention this is because many advisors want new staff to immediately begin studying for their Series 7 registration or Life & Health license, if they didn't come into the organization with these credentials. I think this is a mistake. If you hired a smart but inexperienced person, there's a ton of stuff to learn. Our business is like learning a foreign language—it takes time. For this reason, I suggest waiting six months before having employees get licensed. I recommend waiting twelve months before having employees pursue industry designations like the CFP®, Registered ParaPlanner or CFA.

Who Pays for Licensing?

Many advisors ask me who should pay for licensing – the employee or the employer? On this point, I have a very strong opinion. If you are requiring the employee to become licensed or to obtain a specific designation and if the employee is not in also in personal production, then you – the employer – must bear the cost. Think about it this way…

If you purchased a new data base program for your business and the vendor offered a two day training course for an added fee, you would ever expect your employee to pay for this training? Licensing is no different.

Conclusion

Training is a currency because employees *want* to excel at their jobs. And the bulk of training occurs during the window in which new employees are both most impressionable and most vulnerable. Having a training structure will produce confident employees who learned the important stuff and the right skills from day one.

Let our industry's weakness in this area be your strength. The training systems you just learned are simple, but they will put you miles ahead of your peers.

Currency #4

Delegation

Employees appreciate good managers. But what is a "good" manager? Certainly, an employer who utilizes the currencies we've discussed thus far…one who pays well, trains well, provides a career path… is on the road to being a pretty darn good boss. But the currency I'm about to discuss is more specific in its scope. This currency is designed, not just to make you a good boss, but also to make you good at that one thing you hate most, management. And while becoming a better manager will be one of the ten currencies your staff most notices and appreciates—we're hardly doing it just for them. We're doing it because there is one skill required in management that towers over all others, a skill that will define the quality of the work your staff delivers and the degree of freedom you enjoy. This critical skill is *delegation*.

Almost everyone struggles with delegation. The type of struggle and the degree to which it impedes the business varies. There are the micro-managers who need their fingerprint on every document; the "drive-by" delegators who shoot work at employees then speed off; the "boomerang" delegators who delegate tasks but who invariably feel compelled to snatch them back. The list goes on, and they've all got their rationales and excuses for why delegation doesn't work. Maybe some of these sound familiar:

"I can do it better."

"I can do it faster."

"They won't do it the way I want it done."

And, of course: *"By the time I show them, I can do it myself."*

Underneath all these excuses is probably one simple fact. Most people struggle with relinquishing control. The results of this struggle are lethal. When strong people are micro-managed they get frustrated and leave; when weak people are micro-managed they learn to sit around and wait for you to tell them what to do and how to do it. And when advisors are poor delegators, they grow more disenchanted every year because work isn't fun. So here's the deal. I'm not here to beat you up over your management skills. After all, why try turning a thoroughbred financial advisor into something other than a lean, mean client-building machine? But you can't get to where you want to be unless you learn to delegate, so all I'm going to try to do is arm you with good enough delegation skills.

The Keys to Delegation

Before we can really get into the process of delegating, we first need to understand exactly what the word means. Webster's _Dictionary of Flawed Financial Advisor Logic_ defines it as follows:

del·e·ga·tion [del-i-**gey**-sh*uh* n]

–noun

Giving a task you hate to someone you can't stand.

Synonyms – excruciation; torment; see also _sadism_

I wish Webster would quit publishing that damn dictionary! Anyway, we're tearing this page out. One of the reasons delegation gets this bad rap is because we often jump to the conclusion that a delegated task is, by its very nature, undesirable. But that isn't the case. Delegation is a win-win relationship between manger and staff. It relieves the delegator of time consuming tasks, while giving the employee an opportunity to stretch and grow. Remember, many of the everyday duties you perform that have become old hat can be exciting new challenges to your staff. Delegation _is_ a currency…intelligent employees want to learn new things and grow in responsibility.

So what exactly is the proper way to assign tasks, follow up, and make sure they're completed to your satisfaction? What follows is _Deleg8_™, an eight-step crash course I've developed for the delegation-impaired. We'll learn the steps and by the time we're done you'll be up and delegating like a pro without having to take your eyes off your primary roles of business development and client management.

Step 1: Know what to delegate.

Not sure which tasks to hang on to and which to pass off? Let me help you out here. Pretty much everything you do that isn't a revenue producing activity can and should be delegated to someone else. This includes routine tasks you hate – paperwork, compliance and filing – but also includes tasks you may enjoy – analysis, research or event coordination.

Step 2: Know to whom you should delegate.

A lot of people get tripped up with this one, believing that they should delegate to the person with the most experience to perform the task. On the surface this may seem logical, but the result is often a lopsided distribution of work with one experienced staff person becoming over-loaded and several other capable people waiting, often with frustration, on the bench. The solution is to delegate the task down as far as you can – selecting a person not because of experience but because of ability. Don't have your Practice Manager order lunch for a meeting just because she knows what food you like and the new assistant doesn't. Your Practice Manager is too high on the totem pole and his or her time needs to be leveraged, just like yours. Delegating to inexperienced but eager employees may result in a few do-over's but the payoff will be improved leverage, more cross training and a less vulnerable practice.

Step 3: Start small.

The main reason to take it slow at first isn't that your staff can't handle more…it's that you aren't a natural delegator and we wouldn't want you handing over massive projects the day you finish this book. So start small and work your way up. One of the first tasks you should delegate is one that many advisors hold onto for dear life - scheduling. This task requires no technical knowledge but advisors are often reluctant to let others set client appointments and manage their calendars. Let it go! Another piece of low hanging delegation fruit is coordination of client events. I'm guessing someone on your staff has thrown a party before. Why not let them take care of the nuts and bolts of your upcoming client golf tournament? It's not like you need a full-blown Concierge to do it—give your Administrative Assistant a shot at it and find out if he or she has Concierge DNA.

Step 4: Apply the appropriate degree of delegation.

The very common result of ineffective delegation is unmet expectations. You gave them a task, they didn't do it right, and you never delegated that task again. Sometimes this even happens when you delegate a reasonable task to someone with the right talents to perform it. So what happened? Perhaps you had the right task/talent match, but failed to apply the appropriate level of control. As you can see in the diagram to the right, there are *five degrees*

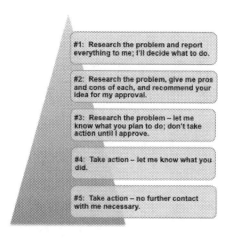

#1: Research the problem and report everything to me; I'll decide what to do.

#2: Research the problem, give me pros and cons of each, and recommend your idea for my approval.

#3: Research the problem – let me know what you plan to do; don't take action until I approve.

#4: Take action – let me know what you did.

#5: Take action – no further contact with me necessary.

of delegation. These degrees range from the tightest control - "Do this, do it this way, show it to me while you're working on it, I'll decide if it's good to go," to the loosest: "Just handle it!" The point to keep in mind here is that you may have an employee who requires only the loosest degree on one task, but needs the tightest on another. Which is fine…whether it's an employee's first day or their 1,000[th], there will be things they know and things they haven't learned yet. It's *your* job to know what degree of delegation to apply. And if you don't know, just ask the employee and let them tell you. Feel free to show them the five degrees and ask, knowing what they do about the task, which degree seems most appropriate.

Step 5: Delegate the big picture.

Wherever possible, let your people own a project start to finish or at least their piece of the project. I never met a smart, empowered employee who said they enjoyed receiving a delegated task without understanding it in its larger context. Instead, what they tell me is, "Lauren, if he shared more at the outset, I could anticipate what needs to get done and I'd do it." Smart people appreciate knowing not only the "what," but the "why." Advisors who would never dream of saying to a client, "Just sign here – you don't need to know anything else" say basically exactly this to employees. Enough said. Spend an extra five minutes filling in the "why" behind the task; sharing a little information about the client and their goals, and you'll be amazed at how much more effectively your employees will perform.

Step 6: Create checkpoints.

I know a lot of you are going to be rolling your eyes here…you want to delegate and be done with it. You're saying, what's the point of delegating a task if I have to spend a bunch of time checking up on what I've delegated? Well, it doesn't take all that much time. What *does* take time is to have to have to re-perform a task because it wasn't completed to your satisfaction. To guard against this we create checkpoints, and we schedule these at the moment we delegate the task. Unless you've appropriately used the loosest degree of delegation – "Handle it! You know what to do." – you'll need to build in at least one checkpoint. Checkpoints serve everyone. They help the employee to be accountable; they help micro-managers contain themselves and they force drive-by delegators to pay attention. So set checkpoints for any project you delegate and establish what components or steps in the delegated project should be completed by those dates.

Step 7: Let go.

Management gurus refer to delegated tasks as "monkeys." Once you get a monkey off your back, you never, never take it back. You can offer suggestions for taming the monkey, you can empathize that that's one tough little monkey, but you must never, ever take the monkey back. Once you do, *you've* become the employee and the employee has become the manager – and a useless one at that. Taking back delegated tasks guarantees mediocrity, uninspired employees and one very over-worked and beleaguered advisor.

Letting go of monkeys also involves accepting the fact that not everyone will do it your way. I've had to bite my tongue hundreds of times as I watched someone perform a task a different way than I knew it should be performed. And you know what? Sometimes this was a learning moment for the employee but, more often, it was a learning moment for me. I've learned my way isn't the only way. By not interfering, I've gotten results I couldn't have achieved on my own.

Step 8: If it's done well, compliment it; if it's done poorly, send it back.

Okay, so you delegated a task, and now it's done. Was it completed to your satisfaction? If the work is shoddy or incomplete, don't accept it. Doing so is only going to reinforce your belief that it's impossible to delegate. Of course, there are scenarios where sending a project back is not a good idea—if somebody is completely overwhelmed by a task, you may have picked the wrong task/talent match. Use your better judgment. But in general, if the person you delegated to has the ability, and the parameters of the task were realistic, and you provided good coaching and resources and you provided ample time for completion, then absolutely do not accept sub-standard work.

On the flip side of the coin, when a task is done well, end the delegation process with a compliment. This is how you build confidence in your employees, allowing you to delegate bigger and more challenging tasks the next time. If you liked the way something was done but didn't effectively convey your pleasure, an employee may assume it wasn't stellar work and do it differently next time. So be specific and prompt with your praise.

And while your employees are working on all those non-revenue producing tasks you were so happy to let go of, you'll be off working your magic with clients, relaxed and fully trusting that the work you've assigned will be executed accurately and on time. Your staff will be stronger, you'll have control over your time, and all at the minimal cost of using some simple delegation techniques. Who knows? You might even find that, lying right under the surface and waiting to be uncovered, you've had a—*dare I say it?*—dormant management gene this whole time.

Communication

Relax. This isn't going to be the "Kumbaya" chapter. You and your staff aren't going to sit in a circle, legs crossed, passing around a Navajo talking stick. You're not going to have to share the story about how your kitten, Mr. Snugglepoofs, ran away when you were nine. We're not getting into *that* kind of communication.

What this chapter is about is how you communicate – day by day, week by week and month by month – the tasks that need to be accomplished. And our key communication theme is *structure*. The more you structure your communication, the more controlled and predictable your practice will be. I'm going to share with you my top four communication systems. I guarantee that, if you adopt these systems, your staff will produce more work, in less time, with fewer mistakes and you'll spend a lot less time worrying about what's fallen through the cracks.

The Weekly Team Meeting

When I see a practice running by the seat of its pants, always in "reactive" mode and consistently unprepared for routine challenges, I usually discover a practice that doesn't employ structured communication systems to share information and delegate tasks. Instead, they typically employ what I've dubbed, *the closet syndrome*. The closet syndrome exists when staff are kept in the dark until a moment of need, at which point they're whisked out of the closet, used to perform an isolated task, and then put back in the dark.

But in practices that run on all cylinders, a far more proactive approach to preparation is employed. These practices have a discipline of meeting weekly. The purpose of the weekly meeting is to prepare the advisor for the next two week's appointments. Notice I didn't say this week's appointments…if you are holding effective weekly team meetings, preparation for the current week's appointments should have been addressed in the previous week's meeting. That's preparation. Following are the key elements for successful weekly team meetings.

Held on Monday

The weekly team meeting is the time to communicate to your staff what you need, why you need it, when you need it by and to identify responsibilities. I've found that the weekly team meeting is best scheduled every Monday morning. On Mondays, everybody is poised for work and ready for new projects. Fridays, on the other hand, have a more laid back feel. Mondays are important, as well, because psychologically, it gives the team an entire week to complete their work.

Entire Team Attends

If their work supports a client, they should be at this meeting. That means that probably everyone on your *Dream Team* participates in the Monday meeting. An exception to this would be a bookkeeper or receptionist or any other position not directly involved in providing marketing, planning, implementation or service support. Everyone has to be on the same page, everyone has to see the big picture. Communication is a currency because all staff, from the top down, want to understand the big picture, and to the greatest extent possible, want to know ahead of time what is expected. Not clueing them in is like sticking them in a dark cubicle in the basement. Sharing information is like giving them an office with a full sunny view.

The Calendar is the Boss

What do you talk about at the Monday team meeting? Not strategic direction, not marketing projects, not how to work the new copier. You talk about one thing and one thing only - upcoming client appointments. And for each of these you're going to identify *what needs to happen, by whom and by when*. So the agenda for the Monday team meeting is actually your calendar. Your Practice Manager or Assistant (or anyone other than you) prints out copies of the calendar for the next two weeks and distributes them at the meeting.

To save time remembering the purpose of each meeting, I recommend that your team use a appointment coding system. Next to each appointment is a code that tells you the purpose of the meeting. For instance, O = open meeting, D = data meeting. P = plan presentation, I = implementation meeting, R = referral meeting, and AR = annual review.

When the meeting concludes, all tasks related to the next two week's appointments need to have been captured by someone (once again, not you, please) and entered into a single task management system so that they can be tracked by client, person responsible, due date or completed date. Outlook, CRM software, and even an old fashioned manual system will do. And while I am certainly biased towards technology, the most important thing is simply to make sure that these action items are recorded somewhere so that there is accountability in place.

Tip from the Trenches

I learned a very important meeting rule from Brian Redders and Mike Sluhan, two sharp young partners in a very successful St. Louis, Missouri practice.

Here's their rule – No new appointments are added to the current week's calendar that weren't on it when they left work on Friday. The only exceptions to this rule are prospect meetings, which usually don't require much staff support. Any other type of meeting added to the current week's calendar is likely to compromise the team's ability to complete planned assignments.

This simple rule keeps Brian and Mike's team from having to work in "fire drill" mode.

The Daily Huddle

I know what you're thinking. "Lauren, I just got used to the idea of having a regular weekly meeting. Now you want me to have *daily* meetings too? There won't be any time to work!" Well don't get your boxers in a bunch, sport. My version of a daily meeting is pretty quick…just a few minutes with your Administrative Assistant or Practice Manager to get you prepped and comfortable for the day. In fact, the meeting is so brief that the person prepping you shouldn't even sit down. Wealth Manager, Rick Farrar, of Birmingham, Alabama has dubbed this ritual "The Daily Huddle." Here's why he loves it:

He walks into his office in the morning and flips on the light switch. On his desk are three neatly stacked files, which he begins to glance through. As he's doing so, his assistant comes in and says, "Good morning, Mr. Rick! Let's go over your schedule today. At nine o'clock you have an open with Bill Williams of Williams Construction. I've done a little Internet research, and typed up an executive summary for you. I put them in the file along with the MapQuest directions. He looks like he'd be a great client.

"At noon, you have a plan presentation with the Fitzgerald's. We've checked the plan document, and all the changes you requested last week have been made. And at three, you have an implementation meeting with John and Mary Kipling. At the team meeting last week you said you'd be putting them on the XYZ asset management platform, so that paperwork is prepped, stickered and ready to go. I also prepped brokerage account paperwork, just in case you need it. Got any questions, boss?"

"Nope. Sounds wonderful!"

"Delighted. And oh…the Marsten case got approved preferred yesterday after you left. Let me know if you need anything else."

Aaaaaahhhh…the power of the five-minute meeting. Could there be a more simple, more efficient, or more comforting way to begin your work day? I enjoy this blessed experience every day. My right hand is

Karen Connelly and each day Karen starts me off on the right foot by saying, "Good morning, sunshine! Let's see what the day holds for our Lauren!" Even though I typically review my schedule the night before, having Karen run through the day's appointments and priorities really helps me focus and hit the day running.

Monthly Meetings

Remember when I said the only purpose of the weekly team meeting is to prep for appointments on the calendar? You probably wondered when you were going to talk with your staff about other critical issues and opportunities, the scanning project, the upcoming charity golf event, the change in suitability requirements mandated by your broker-dealer and last month's production results. These topics, and many others, are agenda items at your *monthly* meeting.

Monthly meetings are a time to focus on stuff that is important, but not client appointment-specific. It's a time not for *doing* business, but for working *on* the business. In the past, in the interest of guarding advisors' time, I tried to use weekly meetings to communicate client-related tasks, strategic direction, projects and other need-to-know information. What I discovered is it's impossible to get through the agenda and an additional meeting usually needs to be scheduled. Staff leaves without knowing their priorities for the week and the advisor has yet another management obligation on his/her plate. When I started recommending monthly meetings to catch topics not related to appointment prep, everyone felt less rushed and better informed.

"Lauren, did you say you want me to share my production results with the team?"

Yup, I do. Many an advisor has challenged me on this one. They were not comfortable with the staff knowing how much money they made. You already know I'm a believer in incentive compensation based on "Key Performance Measures" in the practice. Well, how could we expect our people to play the game with passion and aggressiveness if we don't share the score with them? So every month, share the "big picture" results with your team. For most, that will mean revenue and client growth. For some, it will mean assets under management. Some months you'll be thrilled to share this information. Other months, you'll feel like crawling in a hole. But share anyway. Awareness of how the firm is doing is a critical component of the communication currency.

I like to hold the monthly meeting on a Friday at 10:00 in the morning and then have lunch brought in *or* take the team out to lunch for a little R&R and bonding. You get fresh ideas in a fresh environment and it's a nice way to show your appreciation.

Annual Business Planning Meeting

To those of you who consistently invest time in preparing an annual business plan, I tip my hat. I suspect you're doing very well. To those of you who haven't gotten the annual business plan religion, I will make a simple suggestion. Whatever day it is today, schedule an *"Annual Business Planning Retreat"* for the week before Thanksgiving. Book a small hotel conference room or a meeting room at your club. Send out an email to everyone on the team to put it on their calendars. Ask your Assistant or Practice Manager to get a temp in for the day. Go ahead and do it.

I've seen hundreds of business planning tools and a few I've actually liked. But the format I'm going to recommend for your Annual Business Planning Retreat is a process I learned from my long-time former bosses, Nick Horn and Ted Santon. They required every man, woman and child in the organization to prepare an annual "DOME." What's a DOME? It's a simple, powerful approach to business planning that that involves for four steps:

D – Diagnose. Look back at the year's results on those Key Performance Indicators and evaluate how you did. Did you meet your goals? What were your victories? What allowed you to achieve those victories? Where did you fall short? Why did you fall short? Did you not set enough appointments? Have enough help? Have enough knowledge?

O – Objectives. How much money will you make? How much of it will come from existing clients? How much from people you haven't met yet? How many reviews with 'A' clients will you hold? How many review appointments with 'B' and 'C' clients will your junior hold? How many new clients will you obtain? Make sure all your objectives are tight and measurable. A great rule I learned about setting actionable objectives is: *Start with a verb, end with a date and have something measurable in between.*

M – Methodology. Okay, you said you were going to make X by serving clients who you haven't even met yet. How are you planning to make their acquaintance? Will you re-implement that referral marketing system and hire a part-time Concierge to run it for you? Will you systematize your client touches? Hire a ParaPlanner to free you from number crunching so you can get in front of more people? The methodology section of DOME is where you identify the strategies that are going to deliver your objectives. And your methodologies should be as measurable as the objectives they support.

E – Evaluation. This is the most important component of the DOME process. How will you evaluate your results? Well, for starters, you have your monthly team meeting. But each person on the team should have individual "metrics" that measure the activities within their jobs that drive results. Perhaps you'll have an accountability buddy or maybe a coach. You need to be committed to constant evaluation, constant monitoring of results because *"what gets measured, gets done."*

I recommend that each member of the team prepare their own DOME and share it (each individual presentation should be held to no more than 15 minutes). Following this, I recommend an open discussion of a pre-selected theme for the new year. The theme might be "Creating a *WOW* Client Experience" or it might be professional development or it might be time management...whatever has the greatest cross-the-board value in your practice.

After lunch, most of the staff can leave. But you and your key players stay to hammer out a simple and realistic plan. When it's all typed up, share it with everyone who attended. We want a high accountability practice. And that starts with you.

So there are your communication systems – the weekly team meeting, the daily huddle, the monthly meeting and the annual business planning retreat. But before we move off the subject of communication, I want to talk with you about a key role you play as leader of your firm.

If you want people to follow you, you have to lead with vision. If you cast a vision for your practice that resonates with your staff; if they feel there is something in that vision for them personally, you will have buy-in. Vision-casting begins as early as the interview with a prospective employee. It gets reinforced both subtly and boldly every day, every month and every year. Armed with a clear vision of where the firm is headed, your staff will be able to make good decisions on your behalf.

By the way, the gauge I use to measure how effectively a firm's vision has been cast is to ask a staff member this question: "If I met you at a party, and I asked you what you did for a living, what would you tell me?" The worst answer would be something along the lines of "Oh, I'm just an assistant." That's not the response of an empowered employee. The best answer I ever heard was from Diane Cole, then Practice Manager for advisor Bill Babb of Raleigh, North Carolina. She answered, "I'm a Practice Manager for a financial planning firm. We work with business owners who have a net worth of five million dollars or more and who care about their families, business, and community. We help them with everything they care about." Diane "got it" because Bill cast it.

Effectively communicating the big picture *and* the day-to-day tasks creates a "one-two" punch that knocks confusion, ambiguity and disempowerment right out of the practice. Your employees will love you for it and *you'll* love the results.

Currency #6

Flexibility

It was twenty years ago now, but I still remember it quite vividly. I poked my head into my new boss's office, flustered, and said, "Nick, my son Adam's elementary school called. He's in the principal's office and in some sort of trouble. I'm so sorry, but I have to get over there. I've finished the budget spreadsheets and the Kick-Off presentation is all ready to..." when Nick cut me off. "Lauren," he said, "why the heck are you still standing here? Get going."

I arrived at my son's school, to discover his math teacher wanted him suspended...for giving her the bird! You can imagine my shock. I immediately sat down with my son, who told me it was absolutely untrue. Well, I believed him...but then again, I'm his mother. We sat down with Mr. Kline, the principal. Mr. Kline was an extraordinary human being and a great leader. He talked with Adam and he talked with the teacher. The situation was chalked up to a misunderstanding. Everyone felt heard. No one lost face. I hugged that wonderful Mr. Kline and went back to work.

There's a lesson I'd like to share here. No, not how to shelter your son and turn him into a lifelong Mama's Boy. The lesson here is this: Nick did our family a great kindness that day by letting me skip out, despite being in the middle of a big project and having only known me for a few months. And Mr. Kline, who was in many ways the "boss" of the school, was equally magnanimous in his handling of the situation. In both cases, a little *flexibility* went a long, long way.

Flexibility is ranked by American workers as one of the two most important components in their jobs. It's ranked higher than compensation, career path or training. Flexibility is about work/life balance. *You* put your family first, and when you make flexibility a culture point in your organization, you're making a powerful statement about your values. Employees are far more likely to be attracted to, and remain with, organizations that share their values.

Let's discuss a few of the main areas where you can use a little flexibility to help meet the needs of your staff.

Flex Time

The concept of flex time sounds like this: Boss: "I don't care when you come in, I don't care when you leave, I don't care how many hours you work, so long as you get the job done."

I know very few practices where this type of flextime works effectively. That's because most practices have a limited number of employees and most advisors need the security blanket of having them physically present. For instance, let's say you have a client coming in at 9:00 am. Before the meeting, you thought about a change you wanted to make to your presentation…but your assistant isn't there because he's on flex time. It wouldn't matter that your assistant worked through lunch or stayed late…you needed him at 8:00 and he wasn't there.

But, there are situations where flex time may work. Some ParaPlanners may be able to do their job largely through flextime, presenting you with quality work done on their own schedule. Or perhaps you've hired somebody to design your website…again, there will be plenty of people who can deliver a solid work product outside the confines of a nine-to-five schedule, or even coming in to the office. But overall? I like schedules. Mutually agreed to schedules. They help create a no-surprise environment, allowing you to be more confident, comfortable and in control.

Schedule Flexibility

While I generally don't suggest the use of flex time, I frequently suggest the use of its close relative, *schedule flexibility*. Let me present you with a scenario you may encounter: Your new assistant of four weeks comes in to your office and says to you, "Mary, I'm having trouble getting the kids ready in the morning - one off to day care and the other to school - and arriving at the office by 8:00 am. I know the office operates on an eight-to-five schedule…but I was hoping we could change my schedule to 8:30 to 5:30." If at all possible, you should accommodate these types of requests. You may be thinking, "But wait...what's the big difference between this and the flex time? My assistant still won't be there at 8:00 if I need her for a 9:00 meeting." The difference is that although your assistant still won't be there at 8:00, you know this and can plan around it.

I have always tried to work with employees to give them schedules that helped them manage work and home with as much ease as possible, figuring a less stressed employee is a more productive employee. I've had situations where, at the employee's request, we changed the starting time from 7:30 a.m. to 8:00 a.m. and where the employee still couldn't get to work on time. I usually will give it one more try with yet a third schedule. If that doesn't work, then the employee has a choice to make – find a way to get to work on time or find another employer. We do, after all, have businesses to run!

Quid Pro Quo

The Latin translation of this phrase is "something for something." In employment practice quid pro quo is sometimes achieved by something called *comp time*. You're in a serious time crunch and need your ParaPlanner to put in four extra hours today to complete a complex presentation you're doing on Friday. You ask if she can work these hours and tell her she can have Friday afternoon off. Sounds fair and logical. But beware. Different states have different laws concerning comp time. Some limit it, some require comp time to be awarded at the rate of time-and-a-half and some states don't allow it at all. After checking your state's employment laws, I would use the practice of comp time as an exception and not a rule. Frequently having to ask your employees to put in overtime strongly suggests you need more help. It is cheaper, smarter and fairer to hire an extra pair of hands then to risk losing employees to burnout.

Outside-the-Box Flexibility

I work with a wonderful practice in Huntsville, Alabama. Hugh and Brian Hinson, a father-son advisor team, have a particularly notable form of flexibility that I'd like to share with you. Their Practice Manager,

Sharon, has a younger brother with Down's Syndrome, to whom she is devoted. Once a month, Sharon brings her brother from the group home where he lives to visit with her and her husband for the weekend. Hugh and Brian encourage her to leave early on Thursday to make the long drive to pick him up. But far more important is that on Friday, Sharon brings her brother into work, and he's part of the team that day. He helps prepare mailings and kits, and the guys joke with him like they do other members of their staff. You should see Sharon's eyes well up with tears when she talks about "what the guys have done for her."

While this specific situation may be unique to their practice, it is a valuable example of how far flexibility can go and how important it can be in the lives of our staff. Get to know your staff, and learn the type of lifestyle flexibility they would appreciate most. If you have a staff with school-age kids, hold a "bring your daughter to work day." If you're open for work the morning after New Year's Eve, the younger members of your team might appreciate a special start time of noon instead of eight or nine. To me this was always a flexibility no-brainer... the alternative is having grumpy, tired employees hating work all day, or just as likely, calling in sick. Why not seize the opportunity to be the kind of person your employees brag about? Flexibility, more than any other currency, is what will have your staff saying to their friends "You won't believe what my boss did for me ."

Flexibility in Small Practices

I know there are many advisors reading this who are thinking something like: "Lauren, this is all great stuff, but I'm a sole proprietor with one employee. If they aren't here, I'm out of business. I wish I could offer all these forms of flexibility, but I really can't afford to." Well, businesses like these are where flexibility is most important. If you have only one employee, and her daycare worker doesn't show up, what are you going to do? If it were I, and that employee had consistently demonstrated dependability, I'd be as flexible as possible and just have her bring the baby in. One reason is that it's better than just having her stay home altogether. Another reason is that it's the right thing to do. But for you, the biggest reason might be that your generosity will be returned to you many times over and for many years.

All the currencies pay dividends. On the surface, flexibility seems to offer a bigger win for the employee than the employer. But in the long term, it glues great people to your practice in ways that some of the other currencies don't. For people like Sharon in Huntsville, it's priceless.

Currency #7

Culture

In a way, much of what we've already talked about in this book contributes positively to the culture of your organization. By providing your staff with great compensation, career paths, professional development opportunities, top-down communication and flexibility you've demonstrated that yours is an organization that values its employees. But when people talk about culture, they're often referring to the "personality" of the company. And much of that personality is defined by the unique extras that an organization provides its employees.

Accounting firms that expect employees to work eighty-hour weeks often cater in three meals a day. Silicon Valley tech firms that want to attract talented young people provide PDA's and ping pong breaks. Big firms provide on-site day care, medical services and even transportation for running errands. The common thread in all these companies is a belief that providing unique perks is good business. Perks keep employee spirits high and foster pride in the organization. When it comes to retention, perks can play a big role.

Your company isn't Microsoft, SAS or Google and you don't have a budget for culture perks. So are you doomed to be *uncultured*? My clients have taught me that the answer to that question is a resounding *no!* The following is a list of distinctive culture points that advisors I've worked with have built into their practices.

Mobile Massage. On Fridays a masseuse comes to the office and performs ten-minute neck and shoulder massages for employees at their desks.

Gym Memberships. Healthy employees are more focused and less likely to get sick or injured so consider paying for gym memberships. Many health clubs provide group discounts. If the gym is in your building or complex, this perk is especially valued.

Catered Meals. This can range from simple "Pizza Fridays" to daily-catered lunches. While it may seem expensive to purchase meals daily, consider this: you eliminate loss of work time from employees driving to and from lunch destinations, and it is a great selling point to any prospective employee. And perhaps best of all: every day at lunchtime there is an impromptu staff meeting!

Bring Your _____ To Work Day. A good old-fashioned "Bring Your Daughter To Work" Day can be a pleasant break from the norm, and getting to know people's families makes for a more tightly-knit organization. But you aren't limited to daughters...we know one practice that even has a "Bring Your Dog To Work" Day.

Community Service Days. Melvin Smith, of Birmingham, Alabama, demonstrates that his business is about more than profits. He gives his staff paid days off to be used for volunteering for the organization of their choosing.

Birthday Celebrations. Recognizing birthdays isn't novel, but it *is* appreciated. Whether it's your company's tradition to crowd around the birthday person's desk with streamers and cake or give the day off, people appreciate being remembered on their special day.

Spa Days. Okay, this one costs some money, but it's become a beloved perk at e3 Financial in Newport Beach, California. Once a year, the staff enjoys a "Spa Day" with each employee pampered with the treatments of their choice and a lovely, luxurious lunch.

Serve up the goodies. On the last production day of each month, several of my clients play waiter. They take ice cream sundae orders from each employee and personally prepare and serve the sundaes at the employees' desks. What a nice way to show appreciation and close out the month!

Conclusion

I've listed a variety of fun culture points that some advisors I know use, and I understand that most practices will not be able to offer all of them. But if you can employ just one or two of these tools, you'll be leaps and bounds ahead of your peers. And by no means should you feel constrained to the ideas listed here. If you're unsure what would be appreciated most by your staff – just ask them! How much you spend isn't what's important here. The goal is creativity, fun, and pride in the firm.

I'll leave you with this: A prospective employee has just walked out of your office after an interview, gets on her cell phone, and tells her best friend, "Oh my gosh, the interview went great! The people were so friendly, they offer a free gym membership...and everyone gets a massage on Fridays!" Let me tell you, this person is *praying* to be hired. And with your distinct and enjoyable culture, they'll also pray they never have to leave.

Currency #8

Don't Be A Jerk!

Out of every 100 employees who leave a job, six will leave for external reasons – retirement, spouse relocation or parenthood. The remaining 94 are simply firing the job *or* firing the boss. This chapter deals directly with avoiding some of the unattractive behaviors that frequently result in getting fired as a boss. And the good news is, in this chapter, I won't be asking you *do* anything. I'll just be asking you *not to do* something. What don't I want you to do?

Don't be a jerk!

Please don't be offended. I know very few advisors who run roughshod over their employees or act like jerks all the time. But I know many advisors who, in the face of unmet expectations, can slip into jerkish behaviors. And you know what? On bad days, I've done it too. And while your high-performing, emotionally grounded employee isn't going to fire you for being human once in a while, any pattern of bad behaviors could cost you the best employee you ever had. Following are descriptions of behavior patterns into which we all occasionally fall. All these negative behaviors stem from unmet expectations. You're expecting your employees to do something at a certain time and in a certain way. When it doesn't happen, you resort to behaviors that help *you* reduce the frustration you feel. The trouble is that these behaviors aren't worth a darn in actually fixing the underlying causes of your unmet expectations but are frequently the triggers for getting fired as the boss. So here's my short list of destructive behaviors and the constructive ones I urge you to use instead.

Assigning blame

Something has just gone wrong - a form wasn't signed, a call wasn't made, a fax was misplaced. Your first instinct is to shout, "Who dropped this ball? How did this fall through the cracks? Why don't we have tighter quality control systems?"

Don't be a jerk! Take a breath and remind yourself that a) you've dropped a ball once or twice yourself and b) most errors and dropped balls are the result of a combination of multiple people and systems that failed to work. Mistakes happen and making one person feel worthless will only serve to paralyze him or her in the future. So instead of demanding to know, "Who dropped the ball?" say "We dropped the ball on this one. I'd like everyone to think about what we can do to never make this kind of mistake again and bring those ideas to our Monday meeting."

Unreasonable Speed of Processing Expectations

Most advisors harbor a belief that there's a button an employee can push so that every delegated task can be accomplished in five minutes. And the faster the advisor moves, the greater the "five minute" expectation. Exacerbating this problem is the fact that advisors are relentlessly delegating tasks throughout the day and rarely can remember the 25 things they've already asked their assistant to handle. So they delegate tasks and get irritated when their staff can't turn the work around instantly.

Don't be a jerk! I don't really need to explain this to you. If everything really did take just five minutes, you wouldn't need staff in the first place, now would you? Stuff takes time because stuff takes time. You need to trust your well-trained people to know how long tasks take, how to prioritize them and how to budget their time. *You* are not the operations expert; the people you hired to support you are.

Making your marketing shortcomings your employees' problem

I work with extremely successful advisors – typically people with net incomes in the $1 to $4 million range. Still, most of them have moments of fear. The pipeline is dry and they don't know where their next client will come from. They see their staff sitting with not enough to do and so they turn to their employees and ask sharply, "What are *you* doing to bring in business?"

Don't be a jerk! "What are *you* doing to bring in business?" might be a legitimate question *if* you have a Director of Marketing on your staff or an Associate Advisor who is supposed to be a rainmaker. But in all other cases, isn't it *your* job to bring in new business? If you don't have enough business, you have three choices. You can go get some; you can reduce your staff; or you can accept the fact that if you staff for your "goal load," then there will be occasional times when you might be overstaffed.

Badgering

This behavior, also known as "beating a dead horse" is really unattractive. A mistake was made. First you exploded (see *Assigning Blame* above). Despite the fact that you made your irritation known in no uncertain terms, you're convinced your employee really doesn't understand the gravity of the situation. So you haul them into your office and, with body language that coveys the message "Could you be any stupider?" you badger.

Don't be a jerk! Getting angry is one thing. It might even be the appropriate thing. But beating someone up and raking them over the coals repeatedly isn't going to prevent that mistake from happening again. What it *will* assure is that the employee never makes a move without your input. Hmmm, just what you need…someone who looks to you for all the answers. Keeping failures fresh is like not taking the garbage out. After a while, the whole office starts to smell. Your goal should not be to drag out problems, but to put them behind you as quickly as possible.

Criticism by email

You just received an email from a client indicating that she's still awaiting a response from one of your staff. You have service protocols! Someone isn't doing their job! You're hopping mad! I don't blame you – this one would push me over the top, too. So you take that email and you forward it to the employee who obviously failed to perform his job appropriately. You type your message on top. It goes something like this:

"Why does this keep happening? I don't want to receive emails like this from clients! I don't understand what you're doing that you're so busy you can't acknowledge a client email. I'm tired of talking to you about this stuff. Respond to the client, cc me and please get this issue handled."

Sometimes, the employee will haul off with a scathing response – pointing out extenuating circumstances or your unreasonable expectations. You fire back a response and a full-blown, emotionally charged email rally is in play.

Don't be a jerk! Words can sting. Written words can maim. Long after the incident has passed the written criticism remains as a sharp and painful reminder. You weren't wrong to feel angry but you were wrong to hold your counseling session by email. The right thing to do is to email the employee or leave a message and say, "I'd like to talk with you at 2:00 today about an important matter." Then, at 2:00, face-to-face, you can share the email, communicate your displeasure, require a remedy and get your employee to tell you how they're going to prevent a similar incident from occurring in the future. Always use email to communicate facts or ask a quick question. Never use email to communicate your unmet expectations.

Tantrums

Something goes wrong, something gets lost, something got screwed up, and the deal fell through. And if it's a big deal the first reaction may be to punish whomever you feel is to blame. A tantrum is a concentrated form of any of the negative behaviors we have just discussed. The icing on the tantrum cake might be swearing, slamming a door, huffing and puffing, or throwing something. I do want to say, here, that my heart goes out to advisors. When bad stuff happens to them, there is often no one to complain to. I can explain to an advisor the merits of *being* a good boss, but they themselves probably don't *have* a good boss. You work for yourself. And you're not always equipped with the emotional or material resources to handle all the challenges you face. So sometimes, when our stress bucket runs over, we indulge ourselves in a little temper tantrum.

But don't be a jerk! My advice: if you lose your temper, apologize quickly and be forgiven. One reason is that if you've ever been yelled at or shamed by a boss…or a coach, or a teacher, or a parent, or anyone…you know how hard it is to work with your heart racing, sometimes on the verge of tears, humiliated and embarrassed. The sooner an employee is relaxed—and forgiven—the sooner they can focus on fixing the problem. Typically, they'll want to go the extra mile to thank an employer for being understanding.

I have never worked for a client who has an anger management problem and there are two reasons I never will. First, life is short, and I choose to surround myself with positive people. Second, I know that I'll be re-staffing the same positions again and again for that angry client, which will be very unprofitable and unsatisfying for me. So I just say "no" to people who indulge themselves in temper tantrums, as will any high-performing, self-respecting employee.

Conclusion

I don't want to close this chapter leaving you with the impression that I'm soft on employees. I've spent my career managing and growing others and I did so in a high accountability environment. So *"Don't be a jerk"* doesn't mean look the other way when employees let you down. It does mean be the kind of boss *you'd* like to have. The one with high expectations, who tells it like it is, but who is always respectful. My wonderful and very wise client, Dennis Pettinelli, has spent his career growing advisors and the employees who support them. Dennis says, "I love mistakes! That's how we learn. Just don't keep making the same ones!"

Beyond dealing with the inevitable mistakes constructively, being the kind of boss you'd like to have involves saying please and thank you, always paying for their lunch when you ask someone to fetch you yours, praising in public and criticizing in private. Simple stuff that ensures your employees never, ever, fire you as their boss.

Support

The *Dream Team* is there to support *you*. I want you to be surrounded by a team of people who believe that your job is to be in front of clients and theirs is to do everything else. But how well your staff supports you has a lot to do with how well you support *them*.

Material Resources

You delegate a large task to one of your employees and you want it done well, right and on time. A great first step is to ask this simple question: *"What do you need to really kick butt on this project?"*

For instance, let's say you give your Assistant a big project to execute — transferring all your paperwork to digital files. This requires, among other things, a heck of a lot of scanning. Well, you can just sit your assistant down in front of your old scanner and set him to work, or you can ask what will help him kick butt on this project. With a little research he might tell you that, yes, he can use the old $100 scanner, which would involve him scanning single pieces of paper one at a time. Or, he has discovered, you can invest in a $1,500 scanner that scans large stacks of papers at the push of a button. Do the math…how many hours will it take him to do it with the old scanner? How many with the new? How much is that time worth to you? If an employee makes a request that is reasonable and makes good business sense, don't hesitate on purchasing the materials or equipment needed to do the job right.

This goes for the small things as well. If it's important to you to have a super-neat, well-organized office (and it should be), then don't skimp on the little things. Send your assistant to Staples and give her/him *carte-blanche-within-reason* to purchase materials that will inspire the team to get and stay organized – label makers, colored folders, binders – you'll love the results.

Personnel

One of the most common complaints I hear (and one that frequently drives employees out the door) is that the practice is chronically understaffed. When employees are doing the work of two or three people, they reach a point where they can no longer even pretend to have control over tasks. So those tasks get dropped or delivered a day late and a dollar short. The advisor gets frustrated and loses confidence in their employee. The employee first gets stressed, then gets mad and then either leaves for greener pastures (if they're good) or stays delivering perpetually unremarkable work.

Sometimes, your support staff needs their own support staff. Now you might say, "Lauren, I hear what you're saying about *The Dream Team*. But my practice just doesn't warrant more than one employee. So that's that." Well, even practices with one employee can and should occasionally recruit and extra pair of hands.

One way is by hiring a temp for big projects. If you have a batch of investment reports to produce and there are some rote tasks involved, a temp could help. If you need to get out holiday cards and your assistant is crazed trying to get business placed before year's end, a temp could help. If the filing has backed up and looks like a daunting task, a temp could help. An investment of just a couple hundred dollars can prevent great employees from "overheating" like an engine you push too hard.

Another way of adding personnel without expanding your actual *Dream Team* staff is by acquiring an intern. Many advisors express an interest in this…and why not? They see it as a way to hire somebody but not pay them. While I fully endorse the use of interns in practices both large and small, I would suggest revising your expectations on how and when to employ them. I know that in many cases you probably can find some kid to help with your filing, but if that's all you want them to do, I suggest hiring them part-time and paying them an hourly wage. An internship should be an apprenticeship – an experience that will not only look good on an intern's resume, but also give her or him an authentic taste of a financial advisory career.

They shouldn't be kept in a file room all day; that's a good way to get shoddy work from a bored kid who leaves in matter of weeks. However, if you let them in on some of the meaty stuff—watching you in action on a client appointment, doing investment research, helping plan a client golf tournament—you can have your cake and eat it to. An intern can and should be doing a fair amount of administrative work, but you owe them a true professional experience along with it.

Also, why give interns strictly grunt work when they are predisposed to other talent areas? It's a good bet any intern in their early twenties is pretty talented with technology. So if you have a tech gap in your staff, put your intern to good use – developing that complex Excel spreadsheet, creating a stunning PowerPoint presentation, or customizing your data base program. In fact you'll be surprised how well smart young people can do at a variety of tasks, and how quickly and happily they take ownership of tasks with just a small amount of direction from you. And, with your training as a "talent scout" from earlier in this book, you may even discover an intern has the genes to be promoted to a permanent *Dream Team* position.

Another role that some practices will require is a Receptionist. Sometimes called an Office Support Specialist, this role adds value in practices where the Administrative Assistant is legitimately overwhelmed with business processing, client service and administrative support responsibilities. A receptionist will generally be paid less than your Administrative Assistant, yet they can take on much of their workload - answering phones, filing, maintaining public areas, sorting mail, performing routine compliance tasks, ordering supplies and forms, making up packets, assisting with mailings, and just keeping the practice running smoothly overall. If you add a Receptionist to your team, make sure that she or he is a people person. This is your "Director of First Impressions," so recruit a person who will make both clients and team members feel welcome.

Emotional Support

The final and perhaps most important type of support you can offer an employee is completely free, but essential to curbing "stress runneth over" feelings in your staff. One of the worst feelings, in work and in life, is that of being alone. We are at our weakest when we feel there is no one to turn to for help. And in the heat of battle, feeling alone often leads to panic. And panic has a range of deadly consequences.

Small reassurances of *emotional support* can be priceless in helping your staff through times of stress. If your employee comes to you with a task and says *"I can't handle this. I have too many other things on my plate. I just don't know how I can get it all done,"* don't respond by saying *"Well, it needs to get done, so you're going to have to figure it out."* Instead say, *"I know it's a lot of work. Let's get together at 2:00 today and put our heads together and see what we can figure out."* The truth is, they might not even need any actual help form you, other than these words of support. Sometimes, people voice concerns just to hear others acknowledge the intensity of their workload and to be reassured that their efforts are appreciated.

You can give emotional support to your employees in any situation. Following are some magic phrases you can use to reduce employee tensions:

> *"If you feel overwhelmed, at any point, let's talk."*
>
> *"This is a big project, but we're going to make sure it takes you as little time as possible."*
>
> *"Is there anything else you need before we get started?"*
>
> *"I think you're the most qualified person on the team to handle this. And if you need additional help, we'll get some more hands on deck."*
>
> *"You look a little stressed. Is there anything I can do to help?"*

When you use the support currency, you're saying to your employees, "We're not going to let you get in over your head." And when employees believe they cannot fail, their confidence grows, and, along with it, their ability to support *you!*

Recognition

I've saved the most important currency for last. We've talked about cold hard cash, career paths, training, delegation, communication, flexibility, culture, how to avoid being a jerk, and support. They're all important but they're not all important to everyone. But this last currency is.

Recognition – the longing to be appreciated for who we are and what we do – is universal. But despite the universality of the need, recognition is in short supply in most employment relationships. According to the Department of Labor, lack of recognition tops the list of reasons employees quit their jobs.

People who are good with recognition know they're good at it. And people who aren't, well, they know that, too. They don't need an employee to tell them – their spouses have already mentioned it! If doling out recognition doesn't come naturally to you, here are six simple tips to help you utilize this extraordinary currency:

Recognition Moments

Some people feel they should save their compliments for big achievements, but I recommend, instead the expansive expression of gratitude. Every day when your assistant brings you a file, helps you find your keys, reminds you that you have to leave in ten minutes… that's an opportunity for recognition. An opportunity to say, "Thank you, Janie, for taking such good care of me!"

Frequent

Don't be stingy with recognition. Today is the day you can make someone feel good about who they are. Consistency is the key. One of my clients, who is really a wonderful fellow, has a very hard time giving compliments but he recognizes how important this is. So here's the ritual we use. Every morning when he's getting dressed, my client puts three little shells we found in his right pocket. Each time he compliments someone—an employee, his spouse, kids or a friend—

he moves one shell to his other pocket. He can't go to bed until he's moved all three shells.

Prompt

When someone has done something worthy of recognition, don't let the sun set without recognizing that contribution. I've discovered that feelings of unappreciation can take root very quickly so recognition—whether it's a "thank you" or a bonus check—needs to happen promptly.

Specific

The recognition should be specific. "Great job" is nice, but so much better is: "Jason, the presentation you created for the Jensen's was tremendous. They loved the ideas and we're moving forward with all of them. Frankly, I don't think we could have landed that case without your presentation."

Public

Most people love public praise. So use team meetings to recognize the contributions of your people. Some advisors have a weekly or even daily email where they share the good stuff and recognize and acknowledge their team's contributions. Here's a very effective technique: pass the praise up and down. "Bill, did you hear what an incredible job Margie did getting the Barringer case through underwriting?" And, of course, whenever you receive a written or verbal compliment on an employee – be sure to share it *with fanfare* at your very next staff meeting.

Hand-written

One of the most cherished forms of recognition is the personal note. My wonderful former boss, Nick Horn, made note writing a lifelong habit. His assistant knew she had to keep him stocked in monogrammed note cards. He'd be sitting in the back row of a company meeting writing recognition notes to the speakers and the meeting coordinator before the meeting was even over! He thanked everyone for everything – the advisors for big production months and the receptionist for keeping the lobby area in tip top shape. I traveled frequently in my role in that organization and almost everywhere I'd visit, I'd see Nick's notes tacked to people's bulletin boards and beneath glass desk blotters. They were cherished. I collected a stack of notes from Nick over the years — recognizing specific accomplishments or just expressing gratitude. But maybe the most extraordinary were notes like these:

Dear JoJo,

Congratulations on being selected as Most Improved Player on your soccer team. Your mom has been telling me how hard you've worked this season. I know that wasn't easy and I'm proud of you, honey.

Love,

Nick

I would have done anything for that boss who did so much for my family and me!

I've found that if you practice an "attitude of gratitude", you can be forgiven a whole lot of other shortcomings. Verbal recognition is free, it takes only seconds to deliver and it transforms lives. It's simple.

The most important things always are.

Conclusion

At the beginning of this book you met "Bob." Bob wanted to spend all his time in front of clients and invested a lot of money in staff. But Bob never got the return on his investment he was looking for – freedom. He spent his career chained to his backroom; unable to focus on doing the work he loved. Bob had the right general idea – that freedom came through delegation. He just failed on execution because he didn't know how to staff strategically and was unaware of the retention currencies he had available.

The concepts and processes in this book are simple, but effective. I've introduced them to countless advisors and have seen them work. If you embrace these concepts and practices I can all but guarantee that you won't end up like Bob. You're going to have a calm, well-oiled practice that delivers exceptional service. You're going to have employees who love you and who are proud of the organization they helped build. You're going to make a great deal of money and, far more important, you'll have the freedom to enjoy your life.

If you hire the right people, grow 'em and love 'em, there's nothing you can't do! I hope that reading this book has provided you with the concepts, confidence and tools you need to write the next chapter in *your* book. Now get out there and do what *you* love!

Your Dream Practice is waiting.

About the Author

Lauren Farasati is the founder of *The Gifted Practice,* a practice management coaching firm dedicated to helping financial advisors build exceptional practices by growing exceptional support teams. Over the past twenty-five years her programs, including *Protégé Power in Your Practice*™, *The Time/Client Gap*™, *Your Dream Team Starts Here, The Care and Feeding of the Boss, Deleg8*™, and *The Producer Group Pre-Nup*™ have transformed practices through simple concepts and systems. She opened the Office of Practice Management at Lincoln Financial Advisors, served as Director of Operations for its largest field office and, prior to that, as Operations Manager for the San Francisco General Agency of New England Financial. Lauren is a sought-after industry speaker and has presented at Million Dollar Round Table, The Society of Financial Services Professionals, The Financial Planning Association and LAMP.